CONNECTED AND AUTONOMOUS VEHICLES

THE CHALLENGES FACING CITIES AND REGIONS

STEPHEN PARKES AND ED FERRARI

Regional Studies Policy Impact Books
Series Editor: Louise Kempton

Regional Studies Association

Research Today, Policy Tomorrow

First published 2022
by Taylor & Francis
4 Park Square, Milton Park, Abingdon, Oxon, OX14 4RN

Taylor & Francis Group, an informa business

British Library Cataloguing-in-Publication Data
A catalogue record for this book is available from the British Library.

Trademark notice: Product or corporate names may be trademarks or registered trademarks, and are used only for identification and explanation without intent to infringe.

ISBN13: 978-1-032-39211-0 (print)
ISBN13: 978-1-003-34883-2 (e-book)

Typeset in 10.5/13.5 Myriad Pro
by Nova Techset Private Limited, Bengaluru and Chennai, India

Disclosure statement: No potential conflict of interest was reported by the authors.

Please visit https://taylorandfrancis.com/about/corporate-responsibility/accessibility-at-taylor-francis/ for further information on the accessibility features available for Regional Studies Policy Impact Books

CONTENTS

CONNECTED AND AUTONOMOUS VEHICLES

The challenges facing cities and regions

FOREWORD

Instinctively, we know that connected and automated vehicles (CAVs) are likely to transform the way we move people, goods and services both safely and efficiently. However, the journey from concept to reality has proved harder than anticipated. While driver assistance systems have become more sophisticated and there have been small-scale deployments of CAVs in highly constrained environments, we are yet to see the full deployment of CAVs operating commercially at scale in the public realm.

In the meantime, there has been consolidation across the automated vehicle industry. Smaller innovators have been absorbed into larger companies that can sustain the required levels of investment to continue progress. Other developers are pivoting their technology to nearer market applications, seeking a faster return on the significant resources that have been spent on CAV products and services.

Whilst we await the deployment of CAVs at scale, their potential to cause radical disruption to mobility has led many towns, cities, regions and nations to think carefully about how their transport system should be configured. Their strategies have also been affected by the additional complexity of trying to address the challenges of poor air quality, achieving a step change in road safety, the push for net zero carbon and the shift in transportation patterns caused by the global pandemic.

This book insightfully tackles how CAVs are influencing policy and planning decisions and explores how futures involving such vehicles might emerge, the extent to which existing modelling tools may be disrupted by their deployment, and how potential benefits may be distributed across society, the economy and the wider transport system. This analysis is vital if we are to obtain and fairly distribute the potential safety, efficiency and sustainability benefits that CAVs may deliver.

Nick Reed ⓘD
Chief Road Safety Advisor, National Highways (UK)
Founder of Reed Mobility
Trustee of Brake, the UK road safety charity
Nick Reed ⓘD http://orcid.org/0000-0002-7794-6123

PREFACE

Cities and regions continue to grapple with a multitude of social, environmental and economic challenges that impact their residents. These challenges have been further compounded by the climate crisis (and the need to deliver on net zero commitments) and the Covid-19 pandemic, which has stretched local government resources even further whilst posing fundamental questions about the role of cities within their regions.

It is against this backdrop that the next stage of the emergence of connected and automated vehicles (CAVs) will play out. Much of the attention on CAVs currently focuses on the trials being undertaken in controlled environments or the range of benefits that CAVs will arguably bring. Yet the prospect of more highly connected and autonomous vehicles also has the potential to be extremely disruptive and present further challenges for urban policymakers. In approaching this Policy Expo, we believed it was important to explore what the transition to CAVs would mean more broadly for cities and regions. Specifically, what might the implications be for those places and stakeholders that are not currently engaged in trials? How will the agendas of those imagining post-automobility futures or seeking to enhance the liveability of their environments be affected by the technological, regulatory and consumer push for CAVs?

The uncertainty and extended time horizons over which the deployment of CAVs is playing out and the lack of resources available might understandably be reason for local policymakers to delay engaging with this issue. However, we argue that it is imperative that engagement happens now so that local policymakers have a chance to shape and proactively plan for the advent of the mass adoption of CAVs, rather than have it imposed on them. It is important that they are enabled to do so.

Stephen Parkes [iD] and Ed Ferrari [iD]
Centre for Regional Economic and Social Research (CRESR),
Sheffield Hallam University, Sheffield, UK

https://doi.org/10.1080/2578711X.2022.2085919

ABOUT THE AUTHORS

Stephen Parkes is a Research Fellow in the Centre for Regional Economic and Social Research (CRESR) at Sheffield Hallam University, Sheffield, UK
✉ s.parkes@shu.ac.uk ⓘ 0000-0002-4379-2058

Ed Ferrari is Director of the Centre for Regional Economic and Social Research (CRESR) at Sheffield Hallam University, Sheffield, UK
✉ e.ferrari@shu.ac.uk ⓘ 0000-0002-5506-7670

CONTRIBUTORS

Aliyu Kawu is an Assistant Professor in the Department of Urban & Regional Planning, Federal University of Technology, Minna, Nigeria

Keith McKoy is a retired Senior Lecturer in Transport Geography and Planning at Sheffield Hallam University, Sheffield, UK

Kelsey Oldbury is a Research Assistant at VTI, Stockholm, Sweden

Rebecca Powell is a Senior Transport Planner at Arup, Sheffield, UK

Marc Schlossberg is Co-Director of the Sustainable Cities Institute (SCI) and a Professor of City & Regional Planning at the University of Oregon, Eugene, OR, United States

ACKNOWLEDGEMENTS

This project was supported by the Regional Studies Association (RSA) through the Policy Expo Grant Scheme. The authors would like to express their gratitude to the RSA for its support provided for our research through this funding. We would especially like to thank Klara Sobekova and Katharina Buerger at the RSA for their support throughout the project.

We are grateful for the expert input from the contributors to the Policy Expo, named on the Contributors page. We also acknowledge the support from our colleagues at Sheffield Hallam University, including Sarah Ward and Matt Smith.

Finally, we would like to express our sincere gratitude to those who took the time to contribute evidence to the Policy Expo, including through the global Call for Evidence and the expert interviews.

EXECUTIVE SUMMARY

Over the last decade there has been substantial progress towards the development of connected and autonomous vehicles (CAVs). As the technology that provides CAVs with the ability to undertake more advanced driving tasks has reached the real-world testing stage, attention is now turning towards how CAVs should be regulated and what their impacts might be on the environments in which they operate. Much of the attention to date has been on test-bed locations, where planning around CAVs is more advanced. We argue it is now time to expand the dialogue to include consideration for towns and cities beyond those early adopters to understand how they will fare, and how CAVs might interact with other important policy agendas facing them.

It remains highly uncertain as to what level of automation will be ultimately achieved and the degree of uptake we will see, and how this will interact with the wider transport system. There are some who welcome CAVs and see them as the natural next step in the development of a future transport system. There are others who are wary of CAVs and the promises they offer around safety and efficiencies. They critique that the technology remains fallible and will pose a risk to other road users for many years.

At the beginning of 2020 we launched a project to study these issues. Our Policy Expo, funded by the Regional Studies Association (RSA), was global in scope and therefore sought to draw on evidence from a range of people and places. We have sought to view developments around CAVs through the lens of local policymakers and the towns and cities they represent. Our interest is in what the impacts on these places might be, and how they might respond. Our work has as a result been structured around the following questions, which are addressed in this book:

- How will the urban and built environment practically accommodate CAVs?

- What problems might arise, and will there be "winners and losers"—if so, who and in what ways?

https://doi.org/10.1080/2578711X.2022.2085924

- How will different policy agendas—across geographical scales or policy domains—align or conflict as the urban environment begins to accommodate CAVs?

- Will policies promoting or accommodating CAVs help or hinder other urban agendas including, but not limited to, active travel, zero carbon, health and well-being, social and economic inclusion, and liveability?

- What do best-practice policy solutions look like, and how can local and regional policymakers plan proactively?

- What will national policymakers and infrastructure providers need to do? And what must be resolved locally?

Our Policy Expo gathered information through several channels, including a global Call for Evidence, expert interviews, case studies and an extensive literature review.

It is evident that countries of the Global North are leading the way in terms of preparedness for the introduction of more highly automated vehicles, although a number of Global South countries are ranked amongst these early adopting nations. At the city and regional level there is much less certainty around preparedness to a transition towards CAVs. Increasingly, testing of more highly automated vehicles is taking place across a range of cities and regions. However, the studies undertaken looking beyond these early adopters suggest that preparedness and the ability to respond effectively to the arrival of CAVs is limited.

Several broader challenges compound to create complex landscapes within which local policymakers must attempt to mitigate the impacts of CAVs. These include the extended time horizons over which CAVs might be introduced, and the uncertainty over the roles they might fulfil within the transport system. If CAVs only serve to reinforce trends of private ownership, then the benefits gained through more efficient driving, argued as a benefit of CAVs, might be lost due to increases in the number of vehicles and the distances they cover.

In addition to these challenges, policymakers are grappling with objectives to enhance the liveability of their cities, but the arrival of CAVs might serve to help or hinder these objectives. Certainly, if the asserted benefits of CAVs—such as increasing pedestrian safety or better accessibility for those with mobility challenges—are realized, then liveability might be enhanced. However, for each potential positive benefit identified there is a counterargument and a concern that it will put vulnerable road users at more risk or exacerbate inequalities amongst the population.

Whilst there remains considerable uncertainty over the extent and pace at which CAVs might emerge in cities, some actions can be taken now to help mitigate against the negative consequences. Indeed, the uncertainty about CAV futures makes current thinking about the potential responses even more important. In many cases as the regulatory environment is being developed at a national level, more tools are needed for local policymakers to better plan for a range of scenarios and, in each, to help mitigate negative impacts. For those later-adopting cities, learning through best practice needs to be enhanced. At present there is informal sharing of information, but this lacks consistency and an ability to respond to an ever-evolving sector.

CAVs have the potential to be highly impactful on the built environment. Whether this is a rethinking of land-use strategies or leading to calls for an enhancement of the digital infrastructure of cities, there are significant cost and resource needs that might emerge. The extent to which city planners engage with this will be influenced by a variety of factors, but ultimately it presents a further challenge to contend with. Finally, there is a lack of public debate about the role we want CAVs to have in future transport systems. It is therefore essential that the public is drawn in closer to this topic and provided with the tools to help shape it.

RECOMMENDATIONS

- **National governments can provide leadership in establishing the regulatory frameworks for CAVs, but they also need to better equip and empower cities and regions to respond to CAVs more proactively.** Governments should provide the tools, powers and resources to allow policymakers to respond strategically to ensure CAVs align with, rather than disrupt, their existing policy agendas. As examples, governments should enable local planners to better coordinate policies across existing municipal boundaries, provide more powers over parking regulations and charges, and ensure that active travel policies and funding are part of any package of support provided to help cities accommodate CAVs.

- **It is vital that the sharing of best-practice and knowledge-transfer activities is further enhanced to provide clear and accessible guidance for policymakers less equipped to contend with the arrival of CAVs.** Standardized, simple guidance should be developed by competent national bodies and be flexible enough to allow for the evolving nature of this field. **Disparate professional bodies will need to work together.** For example, organizations that oversee and support professionals working in transport planning, highways engineering, city planning, housing and urban development, public health, and economic development should work together to agree shared guidance on preparing for CAVs.

- **Countries of the Global South should be brought closer into the dialogue around the development of CAVs.** For many of these countries, the challenges faced in approaching CAVs can be much greater, and they should have a voice in how this field is shaped.

- **The public must be brought more closely into debates around CAVs and what role they should play in future transport system.** Opportunities should be created to use simulations and trials that demonstrate the realities of CAV deployment and the positives and negatives they might bring.

- **Dedicated support should be provided to cities around the digitizing of services and collection and management of data to support CAVs**. Privacy and cybersecurity concerns are a priority, but local policymakers may not be well equipped to navigate these.

- It is evident that if CAVs follow and reinforce trends in private ownership of vehicles, this could be highly problematic for the transport system and lead to increases in vehicle-miles and congestion. **The public needs to be encouraged and incentivized to shift towards shared models of ownership as part of broader efforts to achieve zero carbon ambitions.**

https://doi.org/10.1080/2578711X.2022.2085924

1. INTRODUCTION

Keywords: CAVs; autonomous

1.1 INTRODUCING CAVS

The past decade has seen substantial progress towards the development of connected and automated vehicles (CAVs). Accompanying the technological developments there has been much dialogue around the potential for CAVs to help solve a range of economic, social and environmental issues, such benefits being gained through, for example, greater efficiencies on the road network, increased capacities, improved safety by removing human error, and enhanced inclusivity. Throughout this book, we predominantly use the term CAVs, and do so to incorporate increasingly connected vehicles (CVs) that are common on the road network now alongside more highly automated vehicles that are beginning to emerge. This recognizes the fact that this is a broad and transitioning area of study with vehicles of all degrees of connectivity and automation, having implications for city and regional policymakers (Box 1.1).

A large number of vehicles currently on the road network have some degree of connectivity and/or automation. CVs include those with advanced communication technologies, which might include navigation and entertainment systems linked to mobile phones, in-built roadside assistance services (common in the United States[1]), and antitheft tools such as remote engine stopping and locking.[2]

In 2018, it was estimated that 66% of newly registered vehicles in the UK had some degree of connectivity.[3] This increasing integration of the technology is partly through legislative changes driven by a desire to further increase safety. For instance, in 2018, new regulations in the European Union (EU Regulation 2015/758) were brought in mandating that the vast majority of new passenger and light vehicles must include "eCall". This is a system that detects when a vehicle is involved in an incident and contacts the emergency services automatically.

Box 1.1 Connected and autonomous vehicles

Connected vehicles (CVs): CVs are equipped with advanced communication technologies that allow the exchange of information between the various elements of the transport system, including vehicle-to-vehicle and vehicle-to-infrastructure communication

Autonomous vehicles (AVs): Also interchangeably known as automated, driverless or self-driving vehicles, AVs can undertake driver tasks such as steering, braking and acceleration with minimal or no human input, and are able to navigate the environment and other road users. The level of automation influences the degree of human intervention required

Connected and autonomous vehicles (CAVs): CAVs is a catch-all term used to describe both CVs and AVs. Whist CVs exist currently and may have no automation, automated vehicles will, by design, have some degree of connectivity built in, and therefore AVs and CAVs are terms often used interchangeably

---

Connectivity is also increasingly seen through more use of vehicle telematics, which are used by car manufacturers and the insurance industry to understand (and price) the risks associated with driving. Crowd-sourced data also form part of this increasing connectivity of vehicles. For instance, the use of smartphones and satnav applications, which are used to collect and distribute data on mobility, particularly with the purpose of informing on live traffic data and incidents to enable more responsive vehicle routing.

There are also growing levels of automation available in vehicles being deployed on the road network with driving automation systems taking responsibility for a greater proportion of the dynamic driving task. Such systems include autonomous emergency braking, lane-keep assist, park assist and adaptive cruise control.

As of 2018, 61% of new vehicles registered in the UK were at "Level 1" of the SAE "Levels of Driving Automation", which indicates some degree of driver assistance, including those listed above.[4] In the same way as CVs, much of these driver-assistance measures form part of requirements in new vehicles to enhance safety. For example, in 2022, the European Commission is mandating a range of safety features for new cars and vans such as advanced emergency braking systems, driver drowsiness and attention warning systems, and lane departure warning systems.[5]

Ultimately, it may be possible for vehicles to operate on public roads without a human driver. Some developers, such as Waymo and Cruise (passengers) and Nuro and Gatik (deliveries), are trialling such services. The commercial deployment of these vehicles at scale is likely to be part of a transformative, yet disruptive, change to the transport system. These vehicles remove the need for a driver to be in place, or allow for them to complete other tasks whilst travelling, for example, working or even exercising.

The race to introduce CAVs is akin more to a marathon than a sprint and will include a slow, transitional period with much uncertainty. This uncertainty creates a challenge for policymakers grappling with a range of issues within their boundaries.

1.2 TYPOLOGIES AND IMPACTS OF CAVS

CAVs can be divided into three groups or typologies based on their purpose.[6] First, **passenger transport**, which includes private vehicles, but also shared-use shuttles and buses. Private passenger vehicles are where the most disruptive impact of a transition to CAVs is likely to occur, as far as built environments are concerned. As a result, much of the attention currently centres on such vehicles (Figure 1.1).

In addition to passenger vehicles, a second typology is **freight and cargo transport**. This includes intercity deliveries along strategic roads such as motorways, but also intra-city

Figure 1.1 Passenger transport: (a) Smaller autonomous shuttles are likely to feature in future transport systems. Trials of such vehicles are already underway; (b) Passenger transport will also encompass private vehicles where driver tasks are handed over to the autonomous vehicle.

(a)   (b)

movement of goods. Freight deliveries in urban areas are fraught with challenges owing to the often dense and congested network of roads. Last-mile deliveries are a particular challenge for city transport planners (exacerbated by the rapid increase in online deliveries during the Covid-19 pandemic) but also an area where CAVs may contribute effectively (Figure 1.2).

The final typology, as outlined by Ryan Jones and colleagues at the University of Sydney,[7] is **precinct and facility services**. This typology centres on CAVs that operate in controlled, largely closed, environments such as airports, university campuses or business districts. The vehicles might include both passenger and cargo, and they tend to travel shorter distances whilst interacting with a variety of pedestrians and other obstacles. Whilst private passenger

Figure 1.2 Freight and cargo transport: (a) CAVs might come in all shapes and sizes, including this artist impression of AVs for freight deliveries; (b) Completely autonomous vehicles are already being utilized for 'last-mile' deliveries.

(a)   (b)

transport is likely to post the greatest challenge for policymakers, when these typologies are considered together, the potential disruptive impact of CAVs is substantial.

It is also important to note that the arrival of CAVs does not necessarily simply mean a like-for-like replacement of non-CAVs with CAVs. An introduction of CAVs will not have a neutral effect. Some suggest that the arrival of CAVs will attract more people to private vehicles, thereby increasing traffic volumes. Others suggest that, under a shared model of ownership, numbers of vehicles will decline. There is also discussion in the literature about how CAVs might help to increase accessibility, particularly for those with mobility constraints.[8] It may also prompt a rethink of how road space is used, particularly for parking and whether there are efficiencies to be gained.[9]

This prompts us to think about the broader impacts of increasing automation of vehicles and how this might play out in cities and regions. Dimitris Milakis and colleagues[10] framed these potential impacts under first-, second- and third-order implications, the premise being that the first-order effects of CAVs will have a knock-on effect to the second and third orders.

The authors describe these emerging as a "ripple effect", with the first-order impacts occurring first (followed by the second and third) as the ripple moves outwards. It is important to note that these effects can happen with no time lag between them and there can be feedbacks to previous orders. This is elaborated on by the authors (p. 326): "changes in travel cost (first ripple) might influence accessibility, then subsequently location choices, land use planning, and real estate investment decisions (second ripple), which in turn could affect travel decisions (e.g. vehicle use) and traffic (first ripple)" (Table 1.1).

Table 1.1 Likely effects of automated driving

Implications	Possible effect
First order	Travel cost (cost of vehicle, travel times)
	Road capacity
	Travel choices (miles travelled, modes used)
Second order	Vehicle ownership
	Location choices and land use
	Transport infrastructure
Third order	Energy consumption and air pollution
	Safety
	Social equity
	Economy
	Public health

Source: Adapted from Milakis et al. (2017).[15]

The effects demonstrate the wide-ranging potential impacts that CAVs are likely to have. Much of the focus in the academic and grey literatures, and within the press, has been focused on utopian visions of the widespread adoption of CAVs and the benefits they will bring. The discourse tends to be more focused on the utilitarian dimensions of CAVs, such as regulation, safety and efficiencies.

This type of focus can tend to ignore, or at least underestimate, the wider social impacts of such vehicles,[11] including the effects on other road users (particularly those more vulnerable), and who benefits or who might be excluded. This is also wrapped up in a potentially long transitional period where users of non-CAVs will be forced to interact with increasingly highly automated vehicles in the same road space. Whilst for now the majority of CAVs remain at the testing phase and operate within controlled environments, there are examples where higher levels of driver assistance are currently being used on public roads but with concerning or even fatal consequences.[12]

This reaffirms the point that CAVs do not offer a like-for-like replacement for non-CAVs, and why it is important for local policymakers to be informed about their impacts to better plan for them.

Our intention in the Policy Expo and presented here is to provide a broader perspective on the impacts—both technological and social—of CAVs and how these might play out in local and regional environments. Whilst some towns and cities are leading the way and form part of an "early adopting" group or "testbed locations", for the vast majority, the evidence is that there is a distinct lack of preparedness and knowledge around CAVs and their implications.[13] As vehicles become increasingly connected and autonomous, these issues become ever more pertinent, and this forms the core of our Policy Expo, and which will be explored further throughout this book.

1.3 ABOUT THE POLICY EXPO

In 2020, we launched our Policy Expo with the aim of studying the current state of play with regards to the rollout of CAVs and their impact on the built environment. We had a particular focus on advancing the dialogue around how towns and cities beyond those early adopters might fare, and how CAVs might interact with other important policy agendas facing such places.

The Expo was global in scope and therefore sought to draw on evidence from a range of people and places. We recognize that the CAV field is extensive and multidimensional. The Expo therefore did not seek to be a comprehensive assessment of the CAV market and future trajectories. Several market assessments and horizon-scanning reports have been published to serve such a purpose.[14] Instead, we have sought to view these developments through the lens of local policymakers and the towns and cities they represent. We are interested in what the impacts on these places might be, and how they might respond. Our work as a result has been structured around the following questions, which are addressed in this book:

- How will the urban and built environment practically accommodate CAVs?

- What problems might arise, and will there be "winners and losers"—if so, who and in what ways?

  https://doi.org/10.1080/2578711X.2022.2085925

- How will different policy agendas—across geographical scales or policy domains—align or conflict as the urban environment begins to accommodate CAVs?

- Will policies promoting or accommodating CAVs help or hinder other urban agendas including, but not limited to, active travel, zero carbon, health and well-being, social and economic inclusion, and liveability?

- What do best-practice policy solutions look like, and how can local and regional policymakers plan proactively?

- What will national policymakers and infrastructure providers need to do? And what must be resolved locally?

1.4 OUR APPROACH

To gather evidence as part of our Policy Expo, we engaged broadly with those working across policy, practice and academia. A total of 34 participants in our project provided evidence and input, providing perspectives from Africa, Asia, Europe, the Middle East and the Americas. Participants engaged with the Expo through a number of different channels. These included the following.

1.4.1 Call for Evidence

Recognizing our objective to hear about developments and challenges from a range of people and places, we launched a global Call for Evidence (CfE) in 2021, which ran from January to May. This CfE sought detailed submissions from policymakers, practitioners and academics across the Expo questions outlined in the previous section.

The CfE received 10 in-depth submissions with detailed evidence and sources, including information relating to low- and middle-income countries as well as more advanced economies. These submissions highlighted several areas of concern amongst our respondents. This included public acceptance, safety, infrastructure gaps, and legislative and regulative concerns. These issues and their impacts are explored further in this book.

1.4.2 Expert interviews

We undertook 15 interviews with experts working in this field, whose work intersected with issues around CAVs. The interviews covered a range of questions relating to the Policy Expo, grouped around these three broad topics:

- The accommodation of CAVs (practical considerations, time horizons, what journeys might be most affected and who stands to win/lose).

- Impacts on competing policy agendas (e.g., active travel, liveability and spatial impacts).

- Best-practice solutions to the above (and how these might be disseminated/communicated globally).

Interviewees are anonymised in the analysis presented in this book, but they included representatives from policy, practice and academia, who provided a range of insights that we can report on here. We sought responses internationally, reflecting our aim to examine these issues across both the Global North and Global South. Notably, we were particularly keen to include perspectives that include other road users, and the broader implications on these groups of the likely transition to CAVs.

1.4.3 Workshops

We convened two workshops at successive Regional Studies Association (RSA) Regions in Recovery Festivals (2021 and 2022) to engage academics, practitioners and policymakers in our emerging findings. This provided an opportunity for feedback and the refinement of potential policy recommendations. We also presented emerging findings at the Royal Geographical Society (RGS) Annual Conference 2021, receiving further input to guide the Policy Expo activities.

1.4.4 Literature review

In addition to our primary data collection through the CfE and expert interviews, we also undertook a review of the current literature, which feeds into the evidence presented in this book. This includes both the academic and grey literatures (including policy documents, reports and news articles).

1.4.5 Case studies

Throughout this book you will encounter several case study boxes that feature a specific CAV project or example. The purpose of these is to showcase a range of real-world examples of where and how CAVs are being deployed, and the impacts they have had. We have sought to include diverse case studies from different countries and dealing with different dimensions of CAVs. These case studies include:

- Piloting autonomous shuttle buses in public transport: the case of Barkarby in Stockholm, by Kelsey Oldbury (VTI, Sweden).

- AVs in Nigerian cities: environmental and policy issues, by Aliyu Kawu (Federal University of Technology, Nigeria).

- Creating safe CAV services: findings from Project Endeavour (UK).

1.5 THE REMAINDER OF THE BOOK

The focus of the remainder of this short book is to provide an introduction to CAVs, and, in particular, to discuss what the implications of a transition to more highly automated vehicles are likely to be. We explore some of the key challenges facing policymakers locally and how CAVs might align or conflict with other important agendas seeking to enhance the liveability of cities. We then discuss some of the key components of the response to the arrival of CAVs and the role of local policymakers within this. Finally, we offer concluding thoughts and a series of recommendations for policymakers.

NOTES

1 For example, OnStar in the United States (www.onstar.com).

2 Deng J, Yu L, Fu Y, Hambolu O and Brooks RR (2017) Security and Data Privacy of Modern Automobiles. In Chowdhury M, Apon A and Dey K (eds.), *Data Analytics for Intelligent Transportation Systems*, 131–163. Amsterdam: Elsevier. doi:10.1016/B978-0-12-809715-1.00006-7.

3 Society of Motor Manufacturers and Traders (2019) *Connected and Autonomous Vehicles 2019 Report: Winning the Global Race to Market.* http://www.regulation.org.uk/library/2019-SMMT-Connected_and_autonomous_vehicles.pdf/.

4 Society of Motor Manufacturers and Traders (2019), see Reference 3.

5 See https://www.consilium.europa.eu/en/press/press-releases/2019/11/08/safer-cars-in-the-eu/.

6 Jones R, Sadowski J, Dowling R, Worrall S, Tomitsch M and Nebot E (2021) Beyond the driverless car: A typology of forms and functions for autonomous mobility. *Applied Mobilities*. doi:10.1080/23800127.2021.1992841.

7 Jones R et al. (2021), see Reference 6.

8 Faber K and van Lierop D (2020) How will older adults use automated vehicles? Assessing the role of AVs in overcoming perceived mobility barriers. *Transportation Research Part A: Policy and Practice*, 133: 353–363. doi:10.1016/j.tra.2020.01.022.

9 Duarte F and Ratti C (2018) The impact of autonomous vehicles on cities: A review. *Journal of Urban Technology*, 25: 3–18. doi:10.1080/10630732.2018.1493883.

10 Milakis D, van Arem B and van Wee B (2017) Policy and society related implications of automated driving: A review of literature and directions for future research. *Journal of Intelligent Transportation Systems*, 21(4): 324–348, at 326. doi:10.1080/15472450.2017.1291351.

11 Bissell D, Birtchnell T, Elliott A and Hsu EL (2020) Autonomous automobilities: The social impacts of driverless vehicles. *Current Sociology*, 68(1): 116–134. doi:10.1177/0011392118816743.

12 See https://edition.cnn.com/2021/08/16/business/tesla-autopilot-federal-safety-probe/index.html/.

[13] Freemark Y, Hudson A and Zhao J (2019) Are cities prepared for autonomous vehicles? *Journal of the American Planning Association*, 85(2): 133–151. doi:10.1080/01944363.2019.1603760.

[14] For example, see [AQ5] KPMG (2020) *2020 Autonomous Vehicles Readiness Index.* https://home.kpmg/xx/en/home/insights/2020/06/autonomous-vehicles-readiness-index.html

[15] Milakis D et al. (2017), see Reference 10.

2. THE TRANSITION TO CONNECTED AND AUTONOMOUS VEHICLES

Keywords: CAV transition; preparedness; legislation; innovation; acceptance; infrastructure

2.1 INTRODUCTION

This chapter provides a brief introduction to connected and autonomous vehicles (CAVs) and what the transition to a more widespread adoption of these vehicles might look like. It first elaborates on what we mean by CAVs, and how the different levels of automation are distinguished, to provide an understanding for readers less familiar with the detail around them. The chapter then considers the evidence on levels of preparedness for the actual accommodation of CAVs across different places both at country and local levels. This helps to set the scene for the rest of the book.

2.2 WHAT ARE CAVS?

The technology underpinning CAVs can be traced back through successive developments from the mid-20th century onwards. Vehicles such as the "Stanford Cart", which was fitted with cameras and could autonomously detect and follow a line on the ground, and those with on-board computers that could process images of the road to help them navigate were early precursors to the vehicles considered here.[1]

Development of CAVs accelerated in the early 21st century. Much of this progress—particularly around private and public passenger vehicles—has 1been fuelled by technology and vehicle manufacturers developing the physical vehicles and underpinning artificial intelligence (AI) software. This was in response to both government-sponsored challenges (such as the DARPA Grand Challenge[2]) and efforts by vehicle manufacturers to expand into new markets. As a result of this activity, attention initially was largely focused on the advanced vehicle technology itself, and the abilities (and limitations) of it, rather than the broader environment such vehicles might impact upon.

CAVs can come in all shapes and sizes. The concept of a driverless car might conjure images of sleek, futuristic vehicles. In reality, however, CAVs are already here, and they often look very much like what we see as a "normal" vehicle. Connected vehicles (CVs) are far more established on road networks, owing to their lower technological complexities. These vehicles might simply include an ability to connect your mobile phone to your vehicle's navigation system to receive real-time updates on traffic conditions and route options. Automated vehicles (AVs), which have higher technological requirements, are being increasingly seen on our roads.

Proponents of CAVs argue that there are a range of benefits that the development of more highly automated vehicles might bring. This has been debated across the transport community and explored as part of a range of studies on the topic. These idealized outcomes centre on the potential of CAVs to reduce the number of collisions; reduce congestion and improve capacity; lower emissions through more efficient driving; reduce vehicle ownership but also increase access for those in our communities with mobility issues; and help

https://doi.org/10.1080/2578711X.2022.2085926

to support freight transport, and increasingly the last-mile delivery problem in towns and cities. Improvements in safety (for those both inside and outside the vehicle) are a key driver of EU legislation around this topic. Of course, much of this assumes an ongoing desire for individual mobility and we will explore the different scenarios of private versus shared ownership models in this book.

2.3 LEVELS OF AUTOMATION

At this point, the "levels of automation" are crucial in helping us understand how the technology underpinning CAVs is anticipated to gradually remove the need for a human driver to control a vehicle and navigate it safely. SAE International, based in the United States, have developed the "Levels of Driving Automation" to standardize the different levels of automation across a fast-developing industry. These levels have proved to be influential and are widely referred to across the sector (Figure 2.1).

Levels 0–2 are increasingly present on public roads. Nearly two-thirds of new vehicles registered in the UK in 2018 had capabilities in line with Level 1 automation.[3] Arguably, many of us might not see this as a sign of increasing automation in vehicles, but rather just the result of improvements in assistive technology designed to make us safer. Whilst this is true, it also suggests there is an element of "slow creep" towards the highest levels of automation (particularly Levels 4–5), but little public understanding or debate about the implications of this. This matters because there is widespread recognition that CAVs are likely to be a "disruptive technology" that brings about a step-change in how we travel around towns and cities (and between them) (Figure 2.2).[4]

2.4 EXISTING LEVELS OF PREPAREDNESS

2.4.1 Country level

As technological developments have made the higher levels of automated vehicles an increasing reality, attention has shifted to beginning to explore what preparedness looks like across different countries. The KPMG Autonomous Vehicles Readiness Index (AVRI)[5] examines preparedness across the countries leading on CAVs. As of 2020, this includes 30 countries or jurisdictions (Figure 2.3).

These countries have been ranked in the order shown based on 28 different criteria, which are grouped across four broad categories: policy and legislation; technology and innovation; infrastructure; and consumer acceptance. The KPMG AVRI is a core document outlining national-level preparedness and therefore is worth unpicking further. The four categories

Figure 2.1. SAE "Levels of Driving Automation"

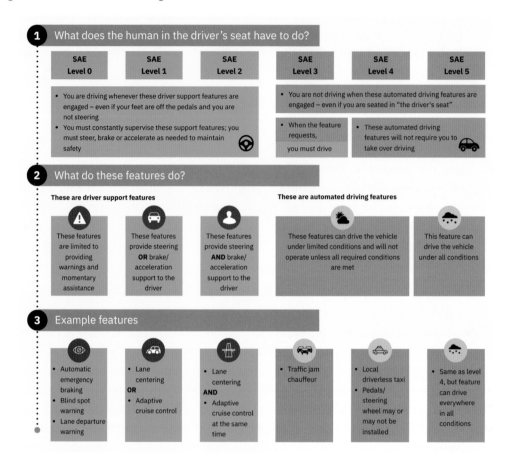

Source: SAE International.

Figure 2.2 Levels of automation: (a) Vehicles at Levels 0-2 have driver support features that can be engaged but ultimately, the driver remains in charge; (b) CAVs utilize AI to assess the built environment and navigate around obstacles. Level 5 sees the vehicle able to consistently drive safely under all conditions.

(a)   (b)

Source: (a) aslysun/Shutterstock.com; (b) Scharfsinn/Shutterstock.com

Figure 2.3. World map displaying the top 30 countries in KPMG's Autonomous Vehicles Readiness Index (AVRI)

are useful in understanding the factors that underpin preparedness at national level for the accommodation of both CVs and, in particular, AVs. It is important to note that readiness here is very much about the creation of environments conducive to CAVs. For example, countries with regulation environments that are supportive of AVs score more highly on this index.

2.4.2 Policy and legislation

This category covers factors such as the regulatory environment within each country around CAVs. It also includes the extent to which governments are supporting pilot programmes, and whether there is a dedicated government agency responsible for supporting a transition towards CAVs. Strategic planning by the government and a readiness to change are also seen as important in this area, as well as an open data-sharing environment that supports more widespread and transparent sharing of data.

2.4.3 Technology and innovation

The extent to which partnerships between different parts of the industry (e.g., between vehicle-makers and technology firms) is important for this category and scores highly where strong partnerships exist. Related to this is the presence of AV firms within the country, particularly where these firms are headquartered, with such proximity deemed important. Other factors relating to preparedness linked to technology and innovation include the level of industry investments in AV, the country's capability to innovate and the strength of cyber security in the country.

2.4.4 Infrastructure

Important factors linked to infrastructure help underpin a country's preparedness for AVs including the presence of electric vehicle (EV) charging infrastructure (essential for EV AVs). Also important in this is the strength and coverage of 4G/5G mobile data networks, as well as the broader technology infrastructure. Finally, the quality of the road network, as poor-quality highways can impact on the ability of AVs to navigate safely.

2.4.5 Consumer acceptance

Consumer acceptance is the final category in the AVRI. Factors important to this include the proportion of the population near test areas. The rationale for this is more awareness and exposure to AVs in active environments increases the acceptance of the idea of them. Other factors include the broader use of technology across society and digital skills amongst the population, which includes measures on individual readiness.

Based on these four categories, the KPMG report ranks the countries by their readiness for AVs, as outlined in Table 2.1.

Table 2.1. Ranked list of the top 30 countries in KPMG's Autonomous Vehicles Readiness Index (AVRI)

1. Singapore	11. Japan	21. Belgium
2. The Netherlands	12. Canada	22. Spain
3. Norway	13. Taiwan	23. Czech Republic
4. United States	14. Germany	24. Italy
5. Finland	15. Australia	25. Hungary
6. Sweden	16. Israel	26. Russia
7. South Korea	17. New Zealand	27. Chile
8. United Arab Emirates	18. Austria	28. Mexico
9. United Kingdom	19. France	29. India
10. Denmark	20. China	30. Brazil

https://doi.org/10.1080/2578711X.2022.2085926

The leading countries offer the most advanced examples of applying the higher levels of automation in real-world (or close to real-world conditions). For example, three bus routes in Oslo, Norway, are now driverless. These countries are also characterized by extensive testing; 81% of people in the Netherlands live close to AV pilots. Advanced levels of infrastructure to support CAVs are also in place, including digital infrastructure.

It is notable that the KPMG list mainly includes countries in the Global North, which is understood as Europe, North America and developed parts of Asia. This bias towards the Global North is not surprising, but shows how developments around CAVs are being driven and shaped by a selective group of countries.

Countries in the Global South on this list, which includes China, India, Brazil and Chile, amongst others, are generally in the lower half of the list, which indicates a lower level of preparedness. This will continue to change, of course. The AVRI reports that China is moving quickly into this area, although this is contrasted with India and Brazil whose AVRI reports suggests there is minimal or slow progress being made. The level of preparedness is very much dictated by national-level agendas. As such, the AVRI largely takes a country-level view and reports on nationwide developments.

2.4.6 Cities and regions

The previous section has considered preparedness to accommodate CAVs at a national level. Whilst the national context is crucial for enabling more effective accommodation of CAVs, the national and local levels are intertwined and dependent on one another. This means it is important to consider the role of cities and regions too. This is particularly pertinent given such places are ground zero for the rollout of CAVs.

Where national-level activity is advanced around CAVs, this invariably leads to increased activity in cities and regions. Places chosen, or promoting themselves, as "testbeds' where trials are undertaken become early adopters of the technology. These cities and regions understand more about some of the considerations for the effective accommodation of CAVs in their local environments. However, a transition towards integrating more highly AVs into the built environment will be highly complex and pose many challenges for both these testbed locations and other cities and regions that have progressed even less on this journey.

To date there has been only minimal research on how cities and regions might accommodate CAVs,[6] although there is some evidence we can draw upon. Research conducted in the United States,[7] which ranks fourth on the AVRI, suggests that there are indeed differences across cities in terms of their preparedness. This work found that only a small number of US local governments had initiated any form of planning for AVs. It was the larger cities and those with higher rates of population growth that were likely to be more advanced in this regard.

Box 2.1   Case study: Autonomous vehicles in Nigerian cities: environmental and policy issues *by Aliyu Kawu (Federal University of Technology, Nigeria)*

CAVs and the informal economy of Nigerian cities

For CAVs to be deployed in Nigerian cities, large-scale urban road expansion and renovation will be required. At present, most urban settlements in the country are lacking functional and well-maintained road networks. This necessitates the procurement of improved and expanded road facilities, and the accompanying infrastructure—as recently undertaken in Abuja and presently occurring in Kaduna and Maiduguri.

This construction and reconstruction is likely to be viewed as attacks on the "striving" informal economic activities that take place in these urban areas. Although the widespread informal economic subsector has been facing increasing pressures for formalization and proper integration, efforts to integrate CAVs will place further pressures on this. Low capital for operation and limited access to shops, coupled with weak law enforcement, has led to these informal sector operators (mainly traders) to operate on and by the roadside. Such attempts to formalize this aspect of the economy in the past have failed, not just because the informal sector is the dominant source of livelihood for city residents, but because the authorities are confronted with the consequences of relocation, resettlement and funding amidst lack of efficient federal and local policy backing.

Processes leading to the rebuilding of existing urban landscapes for CAVs may likely expose the weak structural development controls at city and city-regional levels. These have long allowed widespread unhindered intrusions on roads and similar facilities, thereby incurring additional expense. However, dwindling finances can limit access to the tools and resources to modify existing road networks to avoid serious physical and social backlash that may occur between the formal and informal activities.

CAVs may lead to an end of underperforming commercial and public transport systems, which are dominated by informal commercial motorcycle activities. The current system may also face further policy and city administrative interventions that might altogether exclude them from the city centres and similar areas. However, since large parts of Sub-Saharan African cities are informally settled, this ubiquitous urban economic subsector will be forced to relocate and can only strive in areas largely lacking the requisite infrastructure for CAVs. In places where CAVs are introduced, there may be a boost to more formalized retail activities and increases in revenue as the increased safety and reliability of CAVs help to alleviate congestion and other traffic bottlenecks that often hinder the functioning of retail and viable economic centres.

CAVs: Supporting more effective and affordable urban transport?

Abuja and Lagos serve as the administrative and commercial capitals, respectively, in Nigeria. These are amongst the cities that have been subject to more formalized planning in

https://doi.org/10.1080/2578711X.2022.2085926

recent times. Many other urban areas have been left with minimal planning interventions, particularly in terms of road infrastructure. At present, most residents of Nigerian cities are faced with poorly integrated multimodal transit systems, characterized by high costs, and social and environmental stress. The potential of automation to help deliver a functional, integrated mass transit operation may help to usher in an era of affordable and dependable transit that eliminates the stress of unguided and largely unregulated multimodal city transport for most trips.

Policies promoting and accommodating CAVs

The city of Abuja is known to have more advanced urban development policies than other cities. Along with Lagos, it has become a city where innovative transportation and urban management issues are continuously propagated and easily adopted. Processes of the introduction and management of bus rapid transit (BRT) in Lagos, for instance, has shown similar cities (e.g., Kano) the inputs required and has helped pave the way for overall improvement in the country's urban management policies and programmes. This has helped propel the inclusion of innovations such as CAVs, foster the institutionalization of the entire programmes of efficient urban management in towns and cities, and the phenomenon will no longer be an ad-hoc exercise as in the past.

The development of policies and regulations on CAVs will herald a stronger basis for improved urban liveability through adequate security provision. Proposals for instituting digital surveillance in cities have always been on the drawing board due to lack of finance and the avoidance of infringement on privacy. However, efficient digitization being part of CAVs will help accelerate the process and related matters of zero carbon transport, and the general well-being of urban dwellers.

Proactive local and regional policy on CAVs' infrastructure plan

Local community organizations are people oriented and demonstrate the ability to look inwards for solutions. This helps to give a voice to stakeholders at multiple stages across urban development activities in the Global South. Seemingly intractable issues of land management: acquisition, entitlements and rights, are best handled by these organizations by addressing social, cultural and environmental hurdles that have in many instances stalled developmental efforts by governments and aid agencies. However, by de-emphasizing their roles, many governments and urban authorities in Nigeria are often deficient in approaches known to effectively resolve socio-economic fallout of policy implementations. Hence, the lingering issues of claims of rights, local taxations, differences in price regimes, and policy duplications across regions and cities. This can be avoided if existing and potential trade unions, residence and civil organizations have inclusive and participatory roles in development programmes at all levels; particularly in tackling the persistent policy issues of territorial delineations, infrastructure finance and management, and regional empowerments.

In summary, the development of CAVs in many countries of the Global South presents different challenges compared with locations where the accommodation of CAVs is much more developed. There is a need to formalize and strengthen institutions so as to better support urban development (including road-building) and find ways of accommodating the dominant informal economic activity that is undertaken in cities. Automation of transport may form part of a transition to more integrated and formalized transport networks and associated digital infrastructure. There remain many challenges, however, before this can be realized, and as progress is made the local community must have a strong voice in this.

Furthermore, there was a variation in responses identified based on factors such as political ideology, per capita government expenditures and population density. From an infrastructure perspective, there are acknowledged gaps in levels of readiness of road infrastructure to safely accommodate CAVs in the future.[8] With the process of upgrading road and other supporting infrastructure being long and costly, the risk is that a poorly anticipated disruptive technology such as CAVs can lead to an exacerbation of barriers and undermine other urban policy objectives, such as those related to enhancing liveability.

With much of the activity and "testbed" environments being in Global North countries, the focus gravitates towards them, which is understandable. However, we would argue that this potentially alienates countries that might lag behind with such developments, or whose priorities are not presently CAVs. There are parallels to this problem with other recent technological innovations. For instance, the roll out of fixed broadband connectivity has occurred unevenly. For instance, research from the Asia-Pacific region shows that as improvements in coverage and quality in high-income countries have helped to rapidly increase those with access to it, uptake amongst those in the lowest income countries has remained static.[9] This digital divide is emblematic of the challenge of rolling out new technologies evenly.

Lack of work is being undertaken that focuses on countries in the Global South. The informal road environment, and the economic activities that are undertaken within it, that perpetuates in Global South countries is problematic for CAVs.[10] Furthermore, a lack of standardization for signage and traffic signals, along with significant limitations in real-time data availability, pose further barriers to effective roll out. Motivated by the concern that there is not enough attention being paid to the Global South in the CAV dialogue, we commissioned a case study to provide a focus on a country in the Global South—Nigeria—to shed light on the challenges that might be faced there.

By not including those countries such as Nigeria in the current conversation, there is a risk that progress continues to be Global North centric and at the detriment of a more cohesive and effective transition to CAVs.

2.5 SUMMARY

This chapter has extended the introduction to CAVs that began in chapter 1. The SAE Levels of Driving Automation discussed above demonstrate the breadth of the CAV technology and the step-change that its introduction potentially brings to the existing transport system. Countries of the Global North are leading the way in terms of preparedness for the introduction of more highly automated vehicles, although several Global South countries are placed in the "top 30" of the KPMG AVRI.

There is less certainty around the preparedness of cities and regions in a transition towards CAVs. There is a dearth of information at this level. Increasingly, testing of more highly automated vehicles is taking place across a range of cities and regions. However, the studies undertaken looking more widely beyond such testbed locations suggest that preparedness and the ability to respond to the arrival of CAVs is limited.

NOTES

[1] See https://www.tomorrowsworldtoday.com/2021/08/09/history-of-autonomous-cars/.

[2] See https://www.darpa.mil/about-us/timeline/-grand-challenge-for-autonomous-vehicles/.

[3] Society of Motor Manufacturers and Traders (2019) *Connected and Autonomous Vehicles 2019 Report: Winning the Global Race to Market*. http://www.regulation.org.uk/library/2019-SMMT-Connected_and_autonomous_vehicles.pdf/.

[4] Cugurullo F, Acheampong A, Gueriau M and Dusparic I (2020) The transition to autonomous cars, the redesign of cities and the future of urban sustainability. *Urban Geography*, 42(6): 833–859. doi:10.1080/02723638.2020.1746096; Milakis D, van Arem B and van Wee B (2017) Policy and society related implications of automated driving: A review of literature and directions for future research. *Journal of Intelligent Transportation Systems*, 21(4): 324–348. doi:10.1080/15472450.2017.1291351.

[5] KPMG (2020) *2020 Autonomous Vehicles Readiness Index*. https://assets.kpmg/content/dam/kpmg/xx/pdf/2020/07/2020-autonomous-vehicles-readiness-index.pdf/.

[6] Freemark Y, Hudson A and Zhao J (2020) Policies for autonomy: How American cities envision regulating automated vehicles. *Urban Science*, 4(4): 55. doi:10.3390/urbansci4040055.

[7] Freemark Y, Hudson A and Zhao J (2019) Are cities prepared for autonomous vehicles? *Journal of the American Planning Association*, 85(2): 133–151. doi:10.1080/01944363.2019.1603760.

[8] Liu Y, Tight M, Sun Q and Kang R (2019) A systematic review: Road infrastructure requirement for connected and autonomous vehicles. *Journal of Physics: Conference Series*, 1187(4). doi:10.1088/1742-6596/1187/4/042073.

[9] Economic and Social Commission for Asia and the Pacific (ESCAP) (2018) *Inequality in Asia and the Pacific in the era of the 2030 Agenda for Sustainable Development*. ESCAP.

[10] Pojani D and Stead D (2018) Policy design for sustainable urban transport in the global south. *Policy Design and Practice*, 1: 90–102. doi:10.1080/25741292.2018.1454291.

3. THE CHALLENGES POSED BY CAVS FOR THE BUILT ENVIRONMENT

Keywords: time horizons; ownership; spatial structures; share mobility

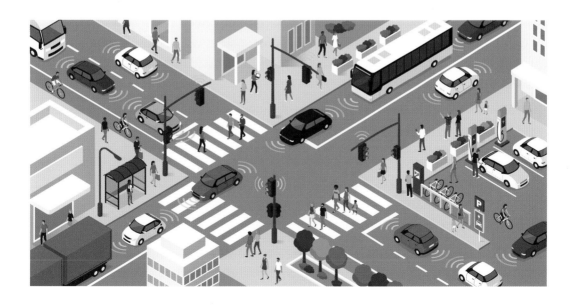

3.1 INTRODUCTION

In the previous chapter we examined how existing levels of preparedness are framed and how these have been quantified to rank those countries that are progressing faster in creating environments amenable to connected and autonomous vehicles (CAVs). We also considered how this is playing out at the local level, which has highlighted that the situation is mixed. Some cities are leading the way and are ideal testbeds for experimenting with CAVs. Other cities do not, or are not able to, actively plan for and consider the arrival of CAVs.

Our Policy Expo was structured around six questions (as outlined in chapter 1) and the current chapter is concerned with the first of these questions:

- How will the urban and built environment practically accommodate CAVs?

As we explore the potential of a full-scale transition to CAVs—with a specific focus on the local level—it is first necessary to understand how they will impact on the *places* where they will be used. In later chapters we consider important factors such as the regulatory and legal environment, and issues such as accessibility and equity. For the remainder of this chapter, we explore in more detail some immediate questions around the key challenges faced in accommodating CAVs in the built environment as they become an increasing reality.

3.2 LONG AND UNCERTAIN TIME HORIZONS, AND THE CHALLENGES THESE PRESENT FOR PLANNING AND DECISION-MAKING

Whilst there is a slow creep of increasing connectivity and even automation being built into vehicles, there remains much uncertainty as to when the widespread adoption of more highly autonomous vehicles (AVs) might take place. More optimistic predictions in relation to AV implementation suggested that by 2030 most vehicles would operate autonomously, although it should be noted that such more optimistic predictions have tended to be made by those with financial links to the AV industry.[1]

The reality is that the time horizons for the development of CAV technology and implementation—to the point that they would have an impact on the built environment which is materially different to that of conventional vehicles—are much more uncertain. It is likely to take many years before the technology is ready,[2] let alone when there has been sufficient uptake for the majority of vehicles to be operating autonomously. Whilst in closed, controlled environments (such as airports or mines) AVs are already operating, the timeline for use on public roads is far longer and more uncertain.

Given this uncertainty, we explored with participants their views about the likely timescales within which widespread adoption might occur. Overall, the majority views were one of some

Regional Studies Policy Impact Books
https://doi.org/10.1080/2578711X.2022.2085927
© 2022 Stephen Parkes and Ed Ferrari

scepticism about the likelihood of AVs seeing widespread adoption quickly (i.e., within the next decade). As one consultant actively involved in vehicle trials put it:

> I do question whether or not these kinds of CAVs that have been trialled, which are for public use like a CAV based taxi service or even privately owned CAVs, I don't expect these will be, you know, adopted and accepted within the next 10–15 years. I do think it will probably take 20 years for that technology to come online.

Even once the technology and supporting regulation and infrastructure are in place, the slow speed at which new cars move through the vehicle fleet means it will likely take further decades before full-scale deployment is realized. An academic put it thus:

> Let's say, we arrive at this magical moment where we have full automation and full connectivity, I think that's at least ten years, if not longer away, then it has to cycle through the fleet so I think we may be at least thirty, forty, if not fifty years away, from such a future and there's significant hurdles that still have to be overcome for these vehicles.

Uncertainty also extends to scepticism over what level of autonomation might ultimately be reached. The SAE Levels of Driving Automation go up to Level 5, which is where the vehicle can drive itself in any conditions, without the need for driver intervention. Some of our participants questioned whether this level would ever be achieved due to the technological limitations that may never be overcome. One interviewee, who has worked closely on the technological side for many years, stated:

> Now, ten years ago, 95 per cent of the problems were solved and everyone thought it was five years away before the next thing was, you know, addressed. But clearly that hasn't happened. The last five per cent of the problem is 95 per cent of the effort really, because it's been increasingly hard to solve the last bits that you really need to solve.

The reason why uncertain time horizons are problematic for local governments is linked in part to the ability to take advantage of the time window before widespread rollout to make sure that the vehicles introduced ensure greater liveability and improve streets,[3] rather than being introduced to the detriment of the streetscape. If AVs are introduced more quickly, local governments may not have the skills and resources to plan for them effectively, and proactively.

Current "testbed" locations will be better placed as early adopters, but these will be the "low-hanging fruit". Often these locations are chosen because they offer uncomplicated road systems, and more consistent (and better) weather conditions. The question is much more about how the later adopters, who make up the majority, are able to anticipate the widespread introduction of CAVs.

The Covid-19 pandemic has prompted some rethinking of the role that CAVs might play in future. This is partly driven by questions around the desire or need for personal mobility to help ensure social distancing. Although as the restrictions have been lifted around the world, this is less pertinent. Perhaps more notable are issues around the increasing levels of home deliveries and online shopping that have exploded since the pandemic, and what impact these have on local environments. Coupled with this is the increasing efforts of some policy-makers to redesign cities and neighbourhoods to enhance well-being and address changes in working patterns.

3.3 OWNERSHIP SCENARIOS

In terms of the role of automation for passenger vehicles, much depends on the type of ownership model that emerges. Two broad scenarios have been discussed.[4] First is the **"business as usual" model**, which sees ownership patterns for vehicles continuing along current trends and where CAVs are acquired and used mostly as substitutes for conventional cars. Specifically, this is a scenario where private ownership and use of vehicles remains the dominant mode. In this scenario, there would be a gradual replacement of non-AVs with AVs as the technology becomes more available and affordable for many users, potentially allied with other parallel technologies—such as electric vehicles (EVs) and charging infrastructure. As is already being demonstrated with EV take-up, vehicle lifespan, fleet replacement policies, product research and development cycles, regulation, financial incentives, and the wider economic environment will all be factors conditioning the speed and breadth of technology diffusion. Pertinently, built environment infrastructure investments which will incentivize and facilitate EV take-up—such as on-street charging or mandating private charging in new developments—and could potentially lock-in the single private owner model of car use for another generation and, with it, extend the dominant model into which CAV technology matures.

There are several possible negative implications of this scenario, however. Those on the lowest incomes will continue to be priced out of private vehicle ownership and, in the shorter term, only those on the highest incomes are likely to be able to afford the first generations of fully AVs. Furthermore, there is clear acknowledgement in research undertaken to date that this scenario is likely to have significant impacts on other forms of transport, especially in the longer term.[5] As CAVs become more attractive and affordable, and particularly if they are prioritized at national and local government levels, there is a likelihood that they will increasingly compete with and potentially undermine public transport and active travel modes. The potential for CAVs to offer some of the benefits that public transport offers (principally, time that can be devoted to other activities), whilst overcoming some of its limitations (principally, route and timing inflexibility), may disrupt the economic symbiosis between public and

 https://doi.org/10.1080/2578711X.2022.2085927

private modes within the spaces in which user trade-offs are considered. For active travel, the conflict may arise mainly on the streets themselves, as walkers, wheelers and cyclists find themselves in competition with a more aggressive and efficient occupier of urban space.

For these reasons as well as the intrinsic status-signalling demand for a new consumer technology, CAVs may herald a potential renaissance of the private car which may challenge the idea that some societies may have peaked in terms of per capita distance travelled by private car.[6] Any actions by national or local governments to support CAVs through built environment measures (e.g., dedicated lanes or segregated kerb space) would encourage further growth in private car use at the expense of public transport ridership and active travel levels.

A contrasting scenario is one that focuses more on **shared ownership of vehicles**. Here, whilst use of CAVs would increase, the overall ownership of private vehicles would potentially decrease as the technology would permit a more seamless sharing of vehicles without incurring the same degree of transactional cost or complexity as with conventional vehicle-sharing. There is much written in the literature about the potential of such a model. Authors have examined the role of on-demand or "door-to-door" services to provide responsive and convenient mobility to users.[7] This could be in the shape of individual "pods" or shuttle buses that offer convenience whilst reducing ownership costs. Within the realm of individual vehicle use, CAVs could enhance the efficiency of short-term hire or vehicle-sharing by being summonable on demand, self-parking when not in use or being used by others. CAVs have the potential to further boost car-club models, which have already been growing in large metropolitan settings such as London where individual car ownership is costly or impractical.[8] Combined with digital platforms, shared service including those offered through CAVs have been conceptualized as Mobility as a Service (MaaS).[9]

From an environmental perspective, this latter scenario is one that is regarded as providing the best opportunity to (re)create cities and regions that better support sustainability goals.[10] In part this is due to reducing the number of vehicles operating in the built environment and thereby freeing up space normally reserved for vehicles (i.e., parking). This is—it is argued—a window of opportunity from an urban sustainability perspective to reimagine the built environment.[11]

Our interviews provided insights into the kinds of questions that cities and regions feel they are grappling with. One interviewee, who is involved in smart cities planning for a UK local authority, described how they saw the question of ownership models:

> There's a whole load of questions around what would the future look like, are we talking about private vehicles? Are these shared vehicles? There's this model about vehicles cruising around cities and people calling them up as and when they need them, and then when they're not needed, they just circle around the city and you know you get all these empty vehicle miles or if they're not circling, where are they parking? So there's a whole load of stuff that needs to be worked through.

3.4 A LACK OF CERTAINTY OVER WHAT ROLES CAVS MIGHT FULFIL

It was highlighted at the outset of this book that the discussion around CAVs tends to centre on private passenger vehicles. Certainly, the focus of media attention and popular discourse tends to emphasize this view. Yet, it is important to keep in mind that the development of CAVs—and certainly much of their potential in the near term –extends to other vehicle types, which might include driverless shuttles or buses, autonomous freight or trucks, and last-mile delivery vehicles.

Whilst visions of widespread CAV adoption might assume that these different types of vehicles will coexist and interoperate at a technical level, there remain many practical questions for policymakers when considering how these can be planned for within the built environment and wider urban systems under "real-world" conditions where the logic of the market might be preeminent. Under the "business as usual" scenario outlined above, other forms of transport such as buses, rail or active travel risk being squeezed out by increased demand for private CAVs. This itself presents a challenge for those wanting to protect alternatives to private automobility for reasons of promoting social equity, environmental sustainability or liveability. In contrast, some literature[12] suggests that under a shared-use model, services such as automated buses and ride-sharing of smaller (automated) vehicles would likely increase, alongside a greater demand for walking and cycling.

Our interviews demonstrated that there is a recognition that it is quite likely that private passenger vehicles will continue to form a prominent part of the traffic mix. However, some respondents argued that it is shared passenger and freight modes where more highly automated vehicles might emerge more rapidly. One respondent working for local government justified this through the alignment of social and economic benefits:

> The reason … is both the societal benefits and the economic benefits align. In terms of the societal benefits, especially in rural areas[,] public transport has the benefit of lower cost per mile even though the capital costs are higher and has dedicated and technical feasibility. It has dedicated routes that you can equip and specific geofence locations. If you're making a vehicle for public transport[,] be it a shuttle or a bus, you're really looking to use it as specific routes and therefore you can factor in the dependencies of a Level 4 vehicle.
>
> This is very good also in the general agenda for cities and rural areas. For cities, because you want a modal shift away from the private vehicle to shared mobility, which would support better and healthier cities, better transportation in the cities, while in rural areas there are a lot of services [that] have been cut because the main cost is the driver, so hopefully autonomous vehicles can support [here].

One of the case studies we commissioned focused on a pilot study conducted in Barkarby, Sweden, on the role of automated shuttle buses. This project looked at how AVs could be implemented to help meet the transport needs of new urban developments in the case study city and involved trialling AV shuttle services and an on-demand service. This exemplifies one important potential role that CAVs can plausibly play in the near term: supporting shared-use options to provide peripheral first/last-mile connectivity to arterial public transport networks. A combination of smaller vehicles, slower speeds, and a quieter, simpler and less cognitively taxing built environment in relatively low densities may suggest earlier uptake. It is also interesting to note that these same environments are those in which the economics of providing traditional "staffed" public transport has become more challenging, further underscoring the potential of CAVs for public transport (Box 3.1).

The second area where respondents felt impact might be realized more quickly was in terms of freight. For freight, the potential role of CAVs extends to both public roads (particularly strategic roads such as motorways and highways) and on private or controlled settings such as docks and industrial estates where goods are moved regularly and repetitively. One of our interviewees, an academic working across different aspects of CAVs and future mobility, considered the potential role for CAVs in freight:

> I think that movement of goods, especially with what's happened over the last eighteen months, is probably something that will be prioritised, the way you control a vehicle that has no occupants and is designed not to have occupants, is probably something that is seen as a lower risk, and it can be operated in ways that you might not choose to be, you wouldn't design a passenger vehicle to move in the way that a freight vehicle might operate, so yes, I certainly think for commercial reasons and for risk appetite reasons, that movement of goods is probably a higher priority in the short term.

This suggests that as a vehicle carrying goods rather than passengers, there may be more appetite in the shorter term to use higher levels of CAVs to fulfil roles within freight.

3.5 THE ROLE OF EXISTING SPATIAL STRUCTURES AND TRANSPORT TRENDS AND HOW CAVS MIGHT IMPACT ON THESE IN THE LONGER TERM

> Autonomous car providers, their kind of "future vision" for how autonomous vehicles would operate in the system and, you know, some of it sounds interesting. But some of it frankly wouldn't be anything that we wanted in [our city]. I've seen people talk about having separate lanes for autonomous vehicles, and again, we just don't have the road space for that, nor would we want it. And you know that we wouldn't need traffic signals because you know these vehicles would just glide through the city, but that affects permeability. So how do people cross roads?

(strategy manager, local government)

In 2018, a collaboration was established between three main actors: the municipality of Järfälla, Stockholm's regional public transport authority (RPTA) and the private bus operator Nobina. The project was named "Modern Mobility in Barkarbystaden" (MMiB). Barkarbystaden (in English, the city of Barkarby) is a large housing development in Järfälla municipality in the north-west of the Stockholm region.

The MMiB collaboration was set up between these three main actors, as well as two innovation companies connected to the municipality and bus operator. The collaboration aimed to work with new solutions and concepts developing in the transport sector. This focused on public transport for a major urban development project, where considerable new housing construction will take place along with an extension of the regional metro system.

The three main components of this collaboration were:

- the development of a bus rapid transit (BRT) line;
- the piloting of autonomous shuttle buses; and
- the piloting of Mobility as a Service (MaaS).

Within the collaboration, the bus operator had the main responsibility for delivering these three services.

Between the launch of the project in autumn 2018 to its end in December 2020, pilots for various services were set in motion. A series of pilots developing autonomous shuttle buses started in October 2018. A MaaS pilot was launched in October 2019, involving an application ("Travis") owned by the bus operator. The BRT line was launched in August 2020; it follows a route that approximates the connection the regional metro line extension will create when it officially opens.

In the MMiB project context, the development of the autonomous shuttle buses as a pilot was the second stage of a pilot undertaken in Kista, another area of Stockholm. Unlike the previous pilot, this time the buses were tested directly within the bus network, because a clause in the procurement contract for bus services allowed for the piloting of new ideas during the contract period.

The autonomous shuttle buses were launched in October 2018 as a limited service provided in the local area under development in Barkarby. During the following two years the service developed in a series of pilots, and as the technology advanced the route was extended and altered. The technology the buses use to navigate is a combination of navigation LiDAR (laser imaging, detection and ranging) and a localization and mapping system. Swedish legislation also requires a stand-by driver on board in pilots for AVs, ready to take over in situations when the technology cannot manage by itself.

The piloting of this service was motivated as a process to explore the role of autonomous shuttle buses in public transport and investigate how smaller automated vehicles can play a new role in an area under development on narrower streets not suitable for larger buses. This pilot has given the shuttle buses the privileged position of being an experiment taking place within public transport, while simultaneously operating as a service under development. A critical question is therefore where piloting ends and how far the parameters of testing will support the development of automation in public transport.

At the time of writing the pilot is set to continue and has received new funding from the Swedish Innovation Agency to continue the development of autonomous shuttle services in Barkarby. This time there is a new focus on developing on-demand services in public transport. The aim of the project is to develop the processes to operate the shuttles via a control tower without a standby driver on board. The new project, named FOKA, will focus on the different chain of events from a person ordering the on-demand service to the arrival of the bus at their location. This project includes the same actors involved in the MMiB project as well as researchers from the Royal Institute of Technology in Stockholm. New partners involved include a telecom operator, working with how information is sent between the sensors installed on the buses and a control tower (e.g., questions of security), as well as an organization working with cloud-based video surveillance.

Overall, the MMiB collaboration builds upon existing relationships and responsibilities connected to public transport. For instance, the bus operator involved in this case was already the operator of more "ordinary" services, providing public transport for the municipality in question procured by Stockholm's RPTA. While the actors themselves are not new, the project context marks a separation from the usual patterns of working. The focus around new services is also (relatively) new territory for the actors involved. The relationship between the automated shuttles and the existing procurement contract is significant in this case as an example of how an existing policy tool (the procurement contract) is used to facilitate the development of new technologies within an existing contract. This case additionally illustrates the influential role the bus operator holds in terms of driving and shaping the development of automation in public transport.

Cities and regions have been shaped and reshaped over centuries in order to accommodate new forms of transport—indeed transport options and technologies have been significant drivers for the locations and initial growth of many of the world's principal metropolises. The existing spatial structure of the built environment and transport trends will be crucial considerations for understanding how the adoption of CAVs will play out in real-world urban and rural contexts (Figure 3.1).

Figure 3.1 The fundamental differences in urban scale revealed by these 2-km radius figure-ground plans exemplify the challenges in accommodating segregated CAV infrastructure in some urban environments

York, United Kingdom   Las Vegas, United States

Source: Authors using *figuregrounder*, from hanshack.com. Data © OpenStreetMaps contributors

To some extent, the relationship that CAVs will have with humans and their built environments will relate to transport dependencies that already exist with the urban context and that could therefore be further reinforced. For instance, it is argued that places that are traditionally more dependent on vehicles and offer fewer alternative transport options will find their populations more willing to travel further as a result of CAVs.[13] This contrasts with places that have sought—or have needed—to offer a more diverse transport system where significant investments have also been made into other modes such as public transport, walking and cycling. These places are seen as more likely to continue to offer a more diverse set of transport modes to their population, reflecting diverse social and economic needs as well as the requirements to service very large trip generators (such as in dense central employment districts).

The development of these urban models and the legacy transport systems serving them have been driven by planning policy as well as the politics and practices of investment in the development of the built environment. In particular, the pattern of spatial relations between points of origin and demand in the metropolitan context—most notably, houses and jobs—will have an impact on the extent of CAV uptake, the types of vehicles that may be automated, and the types of challenge that these taken together might imply. A decentralized spatial structure with comparatively low densities and a dispersed employment and housing land-use model may increase the attractiveness of privately owned, single-occupancy CAVs by increasing the marginal value of time whilst being technically easier to accommodate (Figure 3.2). This may stand by way of contrast to older built environments that significantly predate the automobile

Figure 3.2 Different urban spatial structures could lead to different automation models and imply different challenges to overcome

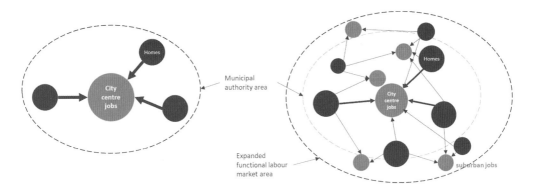

Strong core and artery model
more easily served by transit

- Automation opportunity: public transit reliability and efficiency
- Single occupancy ownership model: shared
- Automation challenge: wayfinding, pedestrian conflicts and kerbside access

Dispersed growth model
more easily served by cars

- Automation opportunity: comfort and multitasking in single-occupancy trip
- Single occupancy ownership model: traditional/private
- Automation challenge: parking, segregation, inter-municipality coordination

age, where a centralized spatial structure based on the traditional city centre may be the norm. In such contexts there may be a more complex and constrained urban environment with more interactions with non-road users, presenting a different set of challenges for planners in comparison with the CAV uptake in a more decentralized structure. Add to this the fact that countries have different legal and regulatory traditions governing road use and vehicle and pedestrian behaviour—with high levels of codification and regulation for drivers and other road users in some contexts and a more informal or negotiated approach in others—including on key aspects of the driving task, such as giving way to other traffic or the actual and implied hierarchies of road users. Again depending somewhat on the age of development of the built environment, road systems may either obviate or otherwise necessitate varying degrees of conflict. Consider the role of grade-separated highways, signal-controlled intersections and jaywalking laws in seeking to minimize conflict and the need for negotiation, and contrast these, for example, with narrow medieval or rural street patterns or the engineered use of shared spaces where negotiation, cognitive heuristics and informal rules become more important. This latter set of cases is likely to present a much bigger challenge to CAV use. One possible outcome if computation progress cannot keep up with consumer demand for, and industrial promotion of, CAVs could be the pressure to simplify road infrastructures and reform legislation to make streets more auto-friendly.

Working against this trend—where CAVs "suit" lower density environments and deliver greater marginal benefits to their residents—we might also anticipate impacts in other types of urban environment. The value of *using* (but not necessarily owning) a CAV—for example, through automated ride-sharing services—could be expected to be enhanced in higher density urban residential environments where it may be difficult or impossible to park a private car.

There will also be significant social and economic gradients to CAV uptake, which may have a distinct spatiality (Figure 3.3). Again, this pattern may vary according to the different international contexts and experiences of urbanization: the archetypical US city with comparatively unfettered development of land together with the sociocultural valorization of automobile ownership has typically suburbanized affluence and residualized urban cores; by contrast, the experience in some major European cities is of a high-amenity, high-value urban core and the peripheralization of poverty. Whilst simply stylized facts, these extreme examples nevertheless demonstrate the very different contexts into which CAV adoption, ownership and use will play out, with radically different marginal utility gains resulting from factors such as workplace location, income, parking availability, public transport quality and availability, and active travel use.

The extent to which the ability of CAV users to undertake other activities will drive demand for their use may in part reflect the maturity and accessibility of existing and potential public transport infrastructure. In situations where there is frequent long-distance travel between dispersed locations—such as in the United States or Australia—CAVs could potentially offer an attractive option for trips not serviced by rail or where air schedules are inconvenient.[14] Alternatively, in urbanized countries such as Japan with very mature high-speed rail networks, CAVs will not likely be competitive against rail for long-distance journeys on either speed or time-effectiveness grounds. In urbanized countries with poor high-speed infrastructure and congested roads, CAVs may be expected to offer comparative speed advantages against rail as well as comfort

Figure 3.3 Different patterns of social deprivation and affluence within cities will affect the extent and pattern of CAV take-up and the trip demands they might accommodate

Leeds   # Liverpool

Ratio of LEAST to MOST deprived 20%   Ratio of LEAST to MOST deprived 20%

Source: Rae and Nyanzu (2019)[18]

gains for motorists, whilst using congested road space more efficiently. In such scenarios, CAVs can be expected to erode modal share from both long-distance rail and conventional cars, whilst automated long-distance bus services may also become an attractive option.

Within urban areas, CAVs also have the potential to impact on how roadside property and kerb space are conceptualized and valued. More use of automated ridesharing and at-home delivery services could lead to more emphasis being placed on property accessibility for loading and less emphasis on on-street parking.[15] Pricing and access control models that, where they exist, tend to regulate parking more heavily than other uses may shift—for example, towards using technology to price vehicle stopping for goods loading and passenger pick-up/drop-off. Irrespective of the precise mechanisms used to regulate future use of the kerbside, the codification necessary to integrate kerb management with CAV algorithms may be at odds with the socially constructed and negotiated norms that have grown up in many local jurisdictions and urban cultures. Whilst this may bring some benefits (CAVs are unlikely to block cycle lanes unless programmed to do so), there is also the prospect of "real risks that the role of streets as places for people as well as sites of curbside [sic] transactions will be lost in the competition for access".[16]

Although the future of CAVs' relationship with the built environment is uncertain and contingent, on balance the fundamental role of the automobile in shaping cities in the past century predisposes them to a certain path dependence. Whilst automobiles have been central to urban sprawl, the prospect of CAVs will assert a significant disequilibrating force on the relationship between housing space/location and travel time, as the value of each shifts relative to the other. Taken thus, and all other things being equal, in parts of the world where urban sprawl has become culturally entwined with lifestyles, CAVs will likely lead to an increase in vehicle-miles travelled, further reduce public transport use and lead to the continuation of dispersed urban growth patterns.[17] This will be particularly relevant under the "business-as-usual" ownership model noted above. As well as changing the form and design of roads, CAVs may plausibly lead to the demand for more road-building, even taking into account their more efficient use of road space at higher levels of market penetration. Even assuming that most CAVs will be EVs, more traffic and more road infrastructure will nevertheless yield negative environmental and public health externalities, for example, through rubber and brake disc particles and the carbon footprint of road construction.

The final set of issues to which we turn relate to public trust in CAVs, in terms of both CAV users and others. Whilst the technology within CAVs can be developed to a level of sophistication and reliability that would permit high degrees of trust to be placed in the operation of the vehicle within the parameters of its instruction set, it will be equally important to ensure public trust in the ways CAVs "understand" and interact with their wider environment. One submission to our Policy Expo stressed the importance of more research into public understandings of place and on public views about CAVs entering the places where they live and work. As they say, "people will not necessarily trust CAVs if these vehicles and the infrastructure which supports them cannot grapple with human meanings of places". This includes perspectives drawn through the lenses of gender and age on issues such as safety, how the built environment is "read", privacy and vehicle routing. Would a CAV slow well beyond the legal speed limit and drive more defensively outside a school when parents begin milling around the school gate? In seeking trust in a vehicle within such an environment, the hardcoding of such behaviours into vehicle software is unlikely to be an adequate substitute for the intuition and heuristics that humans would use.

3.6 SUMMARY

The uncertainties and contingencies that have been noted in this chapter provide a critical barrier for local and regional policymakers seeking to plan for CAVs also make such proactive planning all the more important. Local policy can, to a degree, help influence the role that CAVs might fulfil within a particular city. **However, this is also dependent on external influences, such as national government policy and regulation, or how consumers and the market respond to new CAVs becoming available.** Within the built environments of different cities and regions around the globe, the spatial expression of cultural, social, economic and technological histories as overlain by transport investment and infrastructure will condition both the prospects and possibilities for citizens' positive coexistence with CAVs at the street level. This prompts the need for policymakers to consider how the autonomous automobile, alongside other forms of CAV, might fit into long-term transport plans and strategies at the local and regional levels. Tighter integration will be required between transport policies and spatial planning policies which govern urban development patterns for land uses such as housing and employment—arguably in itself requiring a reshaping of the logic underpinning transport policy appraisal away from seeing transport as something that simply serves inherent or even induced demand to one which fully appreciates transport's role in shaping urban futures and mobilities. To challenge the inevitability of automobility in tension with other urban goals such as liveability, equity and accessibility to services will require political nuance and conviction.

NOTES

[1] Litman T (2021) *Autonomous Vehicle Implementation Predictions: Implications for Transport Planning.* Victoria Transport Policy Institute. https://www.vtpi.org/avip.pdf

[2] Litman (2021), see Reference 1.

[3] Cugurullo F, Acheampong A, Gueriau M and Dusparic I (2020) The transition to autonomous cars, the redesign of cities and the future of urban sustainability. *Urban Geography*, 42(6): 833–859. doi:10.1080/02723638.2020.1746096.

[4] Cavoli C, Phillips B, Cohen T and Jones P (2017) *Social and Behavioural Questions Associated with Automated Vehicles: A Literature Review*. London: Department for Transport. https://assets.publishing.service.gov.uk/government/uploads/system/uploads/attachment_data/file/585732/social-and-behavioural-questions-associated-with-automated-vehicles-literature-review.pdf

[5] Thomopoulos N and Givoni M (2015) The autonomous car—A blessing or a curse for the future of low carbon mobility? An exploration of likely vs. desirable outcomes. *European Journal of Futures Research*, 3: art. 14. doi:10.1007/s40309-015-0071-z; Milakis D, van Arem B and van Wee B (2017) Policy and society related implications of automated driving: A review of literature and directions for future research. *Journal of Intelligent Transportation Systems*, 21(4): 324–348. doi:10.1080/15472450.2017.1291351; Soteropoulos A, Berger M and Ciari F (2019) Impacts of automated vehicles on travel behaviour and land use: an international review of modelling studies. *Transport Reviews*, 39(1): 29–49. doi:10.1080/01441647.2018.1523253.

[6] Thomopoulos and Givoni (2015), see Reference 5.

[7] Enoch M (2015) How a rapid modal convergence into a universal automated taxi service could be the future for local passenger transport. *Technology Analysis & Strategic Management*, 27: 910–924. doi:10.1080/09537325.2015.1024646.

[8] Angeloudis P and Stettler M (2019) *Review of the UK Passenger Road Transport Network, Future of Mobility: Evidence Review*. London: Government Office for Science. https://assets.publishing.service.gov.uk/government/uploads/system/uploads/attachment_data/file/773676/passengerroadtransport.pdf

[9] Enoch M (2018) *Mobility as a Service (MaaS) in the UK: Change and its Implications*. London: Government office for Science. https://assets.publishing.service.gov.uk/government/uploads/system/uploads/attachment_data/file/766759/Mobilityasaservice.pdf

[10] Litman (2021), see Reference 1.

[11] Angeloudis and Stettler (2019), see Reference 8.

[12] Soteropoulos et al. (2019), see Reference 5; Thomopoulos and Givoni (2015), see Reference 5.

[13] Botello B, Buehler R, Hankey S, Mondschein A and Jiang Z (2019) Planning for walking and cycling in an autonomous-vehicle future. *Transportation Research Interdisciplinary Perspectives*, 1: 100012. doi:10.1016/j.trip.2019.100012.

[14] Alkhanizi J, Forrester E, Lyons G and Mackay K (2019) *Planning for Connected Autonomous Vehicles*. London: Mott Macdonald. https://www.mottmac.com/article/58387/planning-for-connected-and-autonomous-vehicles

[15] Marsden G, Docherty I and Dowling R (2020) Parking futures: Curbside management in the era of "new mobility" services in British and Australian cities. *Land Use Policy*, 91: 1–10. https://doi.org/10.1016/j.landusepol.2019.05.031

[16] Marsden et al. (2020), p. 9, see Reference 15.

[17] Soteropoulos et al. (2019), see Reference 5.

[18] Rae A and Nyanzu E (2019) *An English Atlas of Inequality*. London: Nuffield Foundation.

4. ALIGNMENT WITH CONCURRENT POLICY AGENDAS PROMOTING LIVEABILITY

Keywords: liveable cities; road safety; accessibility; employment; environment; health

4.1 INTRODUCTION

The previous chapter considered some of the key challenges faced in accommodating connected and autonomous vehicles (CAVs) within the built environment. These challenges are issues that remain uncertain, yet present fundamental questions around how the physical environment may be impacted by the widespread uptake of more highly automated vehicles.

At the same time as policymakers are, or may be beginning to, considering what impact the arrival of CAVs might have on their cities and regions, they are also grappling with a range of other policy agendas. Several of these are intertwined with the arrival of CAVs and the challenges they may pose, and therefore must be part of this dialogue. These include issues such as ensuing residents feel safe, protecting the environment, providing access to good jobs and services, and promoting a healthy population.

The consensus across the interviews we conducted with industry experts was that the increased presence of CAVs, and in particular the arrival of highly automated vehicles, *could* be highly complementary to these concurrent policy agendas, rather than competing. However, this was often caveated with the point that this is dependent on our ability to detach ourselves from car dependencies and promote more shared use of vehicles. This was summarized by one interviewee as follows:

> I don't think they necessarily do compete, but they do compete if you think about an autonomous vehicle being a car. Most of the evolution of them is towards[,] you know, pods that you stand in for a while and … you can actually get in and out of them and then go off and do something else.

In this chapter, we examine the next three of the overarching Policy Expo questions:

- What problems might arise, and will there be "winners and losers"—if so, who and in what ways?

- How will different policy agendas—across geographical scales or policy domains—align or conflict as the urban environment begins to accommodate CAVs?

- Will policies promoting or accommodating CAVs help or hinder other urban agendas including, but not limited to, active travel, zero carbon, health and well-being, social and economic inclusion, and liveability?

4.2 TOWARDS LIVEABLE CITIES

The agendas outlined above can be grouped around efforts to enhance the liveability of cities. A liveable city is understood as one that has high-quality public/green spaces and built form, has a transport system that allows travel by a variety of means (including walkable

Regional Studies Policy Impact Books
© 2022 Stephen Parkes and Ed Ferrari

https://doi.org/10.1080/2578711X.2022.2085928

neighbourhoods), is safe, respects nature, provides good opportunities for employment, affordable housing, and protects the health of the environment.[1]

Our interviews explored how CAVs might interact with the idea of the liveability of cities and regions. One academic painted a detailed picture of two possible scenarios in this regard, and how these are shaped by policy interventions:

> it really depends on the policies that are put in place for these vehicles because in the interviews we did what came out very starkly was there were some people who said this is a great opportunity for increasing liveability in cities, we can re-shape the use of roadways space, vehicles don't need to be parked, vehicles can be spaced more closely, we could create the downtown or areas where only shared automated vehicles are allowed and so we can re-shape the environment with local regulations and therefore it's going to be a net benefit for everyone because we're leading with liveability, we think about pedestrians, bicyclists, outdoor eating, public spaces, etc. and there's going to be a new urban age around these vehicles. This is the one extreme.

The risk is that CAVs perpetuate urban policies that revolve around automobility and produce the negative impacts that are well understood.[2] The same interviewee highlights this by presenting this alternative scenario:

> the other extreme are the people who say, yes, we have to get the pedestrians and cyclists out of the way, they're going to interfere with automated vehicles[.] I remember an engineer saying[,] well you cannot program one of these vehicles that they yield to pedestrians because pedestrians will cross anywhere and they will hinder traffic flow so what we'll have to do is we have to put up fences, we have to put—go back to the 1050s or 1960s, we have to put in tunnels or bridges, we have to separate the modes to ensure the traffic flow.

As the interviewee summarizes, "who gains from it will depend on the local regulations and how these vehicles are regulated". This clearly has significant implications on liveability in cities, but also interacts with a range of different policy areas being grappled with.

The remainder of this chapter is structured around several important policy agendas, and we discuss how CAVs interact with these. We draw on the existing academic and policy evidence along with insights gained through our expert interviews. The policy areas considered include:

- promoting safe urban environments;

- accessibility and equity;

- employment and the economy;

- energy and the environment; and

- healthy populations.

4.3 PROMOTING SAFE URBAN ENVIRONMENTS

The World Health Organisation (WHO) estimates that approximately 1.3 million people die each year because of road traffic collisions, and over half of these deaths are vulnerable road users such as pedestrians, cyclists and motorcyclists.[3] Many of these deaths occur in low- or middle-income countries where road infrastructure is less developed. In higher income countries, deaths are lower but still represent a priority area for policymakers. In the UK, for example, there are on average five road deaths each day.[4] The annual UK figures include car users making up 42% and a combined 34% being pedestrians and cyclists. Per passenger-mile travelled, pedestrians and cyclists are by far the most vulnerable users (alongside motorcyclists).

Efforts to increase safety on roads is being pursued in part through technological innovation. As was outlined in chapter 1, the European Union has recently introduced legal requirements for minimum car safety features as standard in new vehicles. Other efforts include seeking behavioural changes that can create safer environments for road users. For example, the recent changes to the UK Highway Code,[5] which has created a "Hierarchy of Road Users", placing the most vulnerable users at the top of this hierarchy. The changes have also introduced a range of further measures designed to protect the most vulnerable on the road.

4.3.1 CAVs: a road safety paradox?

One of the key benefits that CAVs, and particularly autonomous vehicles (AVs), might bring relate to potential dramatic improvements in road safety. This is argued because rather than relying on humans to control the vehicle—and humans make errors—CAVs benefit from computerized systems and artificial intelligence (AI) to control the vehicle. This is an argument frequently used by proponents of CAVs and there is evidence to support this. Optimistic estimates argue that 90% of crashes are linked to human error and could therefore be prevented by more highly AVs.[6] Less optimistic estimates still suggest that potentially 34% of crashes might be avoided.[7] On the surface, therefore, there seem to be promising signs that CAVs may indeed align very well with the need to promote safe urban environments.

However, the other side to this recognizes that an increase in vehicle-miles due to CAVs might offset any benefits seen in road safety. It is argued that the increased presence of CAVs might lead to increases in vehicle-miles travelled. This may result from increased urban sprawl or that it becomes more appealing to travel longer distances with less strain on the driver as the vehicle takes on more driving tasks. In this case, the safety benefits gained through automation may be lost by more exposure to risk through the increased levels of traffic. Modelling has also demonstrated that key benefits of CAVs such as reduced collisions and increased throughput can vary according to highway geometry, the ratio of autonomous- to human-controlled vehicles, and to the manner in which vehicle algorithms form "platoons" and the

https://doi.org/10.1080/2578711X.2022.2085928

headway between them.[8] In real-world, rather than laboratory, conditions, such factors will vary so widely that the precise safety outcomes of CAVs may be very difficult to predict.

4.3.2 "Ironies of automation"

At present, vehicles, even new ones, are still dependent on human drivers to be in control of the vehicle, and this is likely to be the case for several more years. Even then, some argue that full Level 5 automation may never be reached. This means that it is likely that, for a long time to come, drivers will have a role to play. Ian Noy et al.[9] explored "safety blind spots" in AVs and identified what they have termed the "ironies of automation". These "ironies" relate to a view that increasing automation may actually place more demands on drivers and lead to more dangerous outcomes for road users. This is partly based on the following arguments:

- AVs will initially take the easier driving tasks, leaving humans with only the most challenging to deal with.

- It will lead to a "deskilling", for example, through lack of driving practice, and subsequent reductions in driving skills and reaction times.

- Less demand for cognitive engagement in driving will lead to lower levels of situational awareness and longer reaction times.

- Less time spent driving and less familiarity with driving the vehicle can lead to poor responses when the human does ultimately have to engage in those more challenging situations.

These ironies are particularly important given the long transitional period over which CAVs will be introduced into the road network. Over many years, drivers, passengers and other road users may be faced with ever more complex interactions with uncertain outcomes.

4.3.3 Overestimating the abilities of CAVs

In addition to these "ironies of automation", further complexities will continue to challenge the ability of policymakers to ensure a safe environment for their residents. One of these is an overestimation of the abilities of CAVs. This overconfidence in CAV abilities can be seen—it is argued—in both drivers and passengers as well other road users, specifically pedestrians. It remains early to draw concrete conclusions as to the extent to which the abilities of CAVs might be (over)estimated; indeed, it depends on the true extent of the abilities (or SAE Levels) that CAVs ultimately achieve.

Some research has explored this. Work by Lynn Hulse et al.[10] in the UK, United States and Australia showed differences in estimation of risk by gender. Specifically, that males were more likely to regard AVs as less risky, although with males more likely to engage in riskier behaviours in the first place this was unsurprising. It has also been suggested[11] that pedestrians may "behave with impunity" with regards their interactions with more highly automated vehicles (e.g., when crossing roads). This is because of a belief that AVs will be "risk averse" and pedestrians will feel more able to simply step out in front of the vehicles and trust it to stop.

Overestimating the abilities of CAVs is embedded in the extent to which you trust them. Using a CAV at higher levels of automation (i.e., Levels 3–5) involves a handing over of control. Whilst ever the technology is nascent, this is likely to be perceived by many as placing themselves in a vulnerable position. In contrast, some may overestimate the abilities of more highly automated vehicles, and this can equally damage trust amongst users when things go wrong.

Research conducted on CAVs has shown that trust is one of the major determinants of the intention to use the vehicles.[12] This research has also shown that the following three elements are strongly linked to trust in the use of AVs:

- System transparency: the AV acts consistently, and its future behaviour can be predicted.

- Technical competence: that AVs are free of making errors, are reliable and perform consistently under different circumstances.

- Situation management: that AVs can provide alternative solutions and effectively respond in situations.

4.3.4 Segregation of road space and users

Much of the uncertainty around the safety of CAVs, and whether they, and other road users, can safely coexist alongside one another, has raised questions around the future allocation of road space. Specifically, the question of whether dedicated CAV lanes should be created in cities[13] or if physical barriers might be erected to separate pedestrians and other vulnerable users from the road.[14]

Segregation of road users is not new and is characteristic of street design of the mid-20th century, as the private car became the dominant mode of travel, with vehicles travelling at higher speeds and demanding more space. Some segregation can be prohibitive, for example, forcing pedestrians to take circuitous routes to their destinations. However, there are calls for additional segregation in certain circumstances. For example, the segregation of cyclists from vehicles (and pedestrians), particularly on busy roads where vehicles travel at high speeds. These debates are central in the discourse around efforts to increase levels of cycling, and evidence suggests that appropriate infrastructure can increase levels of active travel such as cycling (Figure 4.1).[15]

There is some emerging evidence to suggest that people might also prefer segregated facilities in the presence of more highly automated vehicles due to a lack of trust in the vehicles

https://doi.org/10.1080/2578711X.2022.2085928

Figure 4.1. Segregation of road users: (a) Physical barriers to separate users seek to reduce conflict between cars and pedestrians/cyclists, but can diminish the built environment and make it more challenging to navigate; (b) Space can often be squeezed from pedestrians in favour of motor vehicles.

(a)   (b)

Source: (a) Source: LariBat/Shutterstock.com; (b) Source: Tim Roberts Photography/Shutterstock.com

themselves,[16] although the study authors also suggest that more awareness of the abilities of CAVs will likely ultimately reduce this desire somewhat.

The desire for more segregation is potentially problematic as—implemented poorly—such segregation can be divisive and create barriers to more active ways of travelling, specifically walking. Indeed, attention has been paid to how barriers might be removed whilst still creating safer environments, for example, removing physical barriers, signs, road markings and even kerbs. The logic of these efforts is that it forces a greater awareness of, and between, other road users, particularly those in motorized vehicles, and helps to reduce traffic speeds[17] and make the environment safer.

The question mark over the infallibility of CAVs, particularly at the higher levels of automation, might ultimately lead to barriers being put in place rather than removed, and potentially make roads more hostile to the most vulnerable road users. This will be one of the more challenging problems for policymakers to tackle.

4.4 ACCESSIBILITY AND EQUITY

A critical challenge of policymakers is to address issues of accessibility and inequities amongst their populations. This is an existing problem within transport policy and the arrival of CAVs adds complex dynamics to the debate.

4.4.1 Increasing access for those with mobility constraints

On the one hand, increasingly AVs offer those with limited mobility, such as people with physical disabilities or elderly populations, with increased access to services and opportunities. This is something that has been examined by researchers, with the potential for benefits clearly highlighted. For instance, Faber and van Lierop[18] explored intentions of older adults in the Netherlands to use more highly automated vehicles. The Netherlands is currently second in the KPMG Autonomous Vehicles Readiness Index (AVRI). This study showed there was a strong preference for on-demand, shared AVs, which emphasizes the role that such vehicles might have in providing responsive—and sociable—travel options for such individuals.

It is important to recognize that needs—and engagement with CAVs—will vary across different age groups and circumstances. A good example of this is from research by Li et al.,[19] which showed that older people (aged 60+) should not be considered as one homogenous group. Their work showed that those aged 70+ were less stable and slower in their takeover of Level 3 CAVs compared with the 60–69-year age group. Further, whilst the benefits to those with mobility issues are recognized, it has been argued that these users need to have a voice in the debate around CAVs, particularly to help shape issue around design, testing and development so that such users do indeed benefit rather than risk being left behind.[20]

4.4.2 Exacerbating inequalities

Whilst CAVs offer potentially important solutions to issues of accessibility and barriers for some residents, there is another side to this that should be considered. This relates to equity and issues of transport poverty.

In terms of access to private transport, it is recognized that this can be uneven, with those on low incomes less likely to be able to afford it. Transport planning and the systems they produce—across different countries—can, to varying degrees, create environments that mean significant portions of the population struggle to access service due to transport poverty. High costs of car ownership and public transport, coupled with hostile environments for active travel, can lead to many households becoming isolated. In addition, in the face of lower skill and lower paid jobs increasingly being located on the edge of cities (as highlighted by Richard Crisp et al.[21]), more deprived households can be forced into unaffordable car ownership due to the poor alternative transport options. Amongst these trends, Bissell et al.[22] argue that for CAVs, this might be no different: "just like previous mobility systems, access to [CAVs] is likely to be unevenly distributed across classed and racial lines".

Bissel et al. also argue that some automated transport systems may emerge as multi-tiered with regards to the services offered. This could be realized through more exclusive and costly AV services that can travel further, faster, more flexibly, and more comfortably. Even at basic levels of service, the costs may be out of reach for a significant proportion of the population for many years, further exacerbating inequalities in transport.

An argument in favour of CAVs is that they will help to resolve the problem of vehicles using premium space within a city to sit unused whilst their passengers do not need them. It is suggested that they will be able to park outside of these areas where space is a premium (such as the city centre) and return when required to collect their passenger. This is potentially problematic depending on where they end up parking during these gaps. Fábio Duerte and Carlo Ratti discussed this, stating, "AVs could move back home or to cheaper parking areas designated by the city as less impactful to the overall traffic".[23] This raises the question as to what is deemed "less impactful", and who decides this? The concern is that in more deprived areas (which are often located just outside the city centre) are subjected to high numbers of CAVs navigating their neighbourhoods seeking space to park, with residents having little or no say in this.

4.4.3 The burden of responsibility

A further factor relating to issues of equity relates to where the burden of responsibility over safety falls. Whilst all road users have a responsibility towards others, it is increasingly the case that hierarchies of road users are explicitly stated, with those using modes of transport that have the potential to be most harmful (e.g., heavy goods vehicles or cars) having more responsibility for those more vulnerable (such as pedestrians and cyclists). For CAVs, the identification of pedestrians, and particularly cyclists, remains a challenge technologically. One solution, which has been highlighted through recent legislative developments in the United States, has laid the ground for the potential introduction of "beacons" to protect the most vulnerable road users.

This solution involves using technology already inbuilt into smartphones or sensors that could be incorporated on bicycles or worn on the clothing of pedestrians that communicate with CAVs to alert them to the presence of these other road users.[24] This places the onus on pedestrians and cyclists to protect themselves, which is potentially problematic, particularly as an awareness of such measures might make drivers more complacent and less attentive to what is in front of them on the road. As is highlighted by transport journalist Carlton Reid in his reporting of these developments,[25] there are important questions around equity. For instance, what if a person does not have access to a mobile phone or a "beacon"—does this place them at additional risk?

Siri Hegna Berge led some work in this area,[26] specifically focused on cyclists. This found some hesitancy amongst cyclists for the potential use of "on-bike human–machine interfaces" or beacons. Partly, this was driven by a view that the AV technology should be sufficiently advanced to reliably identify such users without the need for beacons before it is deployed on a large scale in traffic. The consensus from participants in this study was that the "primary responsibility of safety lies with the AV". Additionally, this research reiterated

https://doi.org/10.1080/2578711X.2022.2085928

the concerns raised by Reid. Specifically, that such requirements might create barriers to cycling and make it less accessible.

4.5 EMPLOYMENT AND THE ECONOMY

CAVs could potentially have a significant impact on employment and the wider economy. One key area of impact would be on the occupations likely to be replaced, or significantly impacted by an increasing presence of CAVs. These are roles that are directly associated with the operation of vehicles, for example, freight, buses and private-hire vehicles (taxis). Such roles could be significantly threatened by the increasing role of automation and the significant financial savings to businesses achieved by removing labour costs.[27] This is in addition to the jobs across the economy that might be impacted by increasing levels of automation in processes. Whilst new jobs would be created supporting the expanding CAV industry, these would not necessarily be a direct replacement for existing workers, many of whom may not have the requisite skills.[28]

Alongside the impacts on those in "at-risk" occupations, CAVs are also likely to have implications for the spatial distribution of labour and jobs. This could include employment opportunities moving to locations where land is cheaper outside of the city centre, thereby forcing workers into longer and more costly journeys. There is also the likelihood that automation might lead to jobs being able to be fulfilled in different locations to where the technology is operating, again shifting the employment landscape.[29]

4.6 ENERGY AND THE ENVIRONMENT

Tackling energy use and reducing environmental impact is a vitally important policy area for cities and regions, particularly as efforts to deliver on net zero commitments accelerate. This is interrelated with other issues considered in this chapter, such as resident safety, liveability and health.

One of the key arguments in favour of CAVs from an environmental perspective is the benefits they can deliver compared with human-driven vehicles. CAVs, it is argued, will drive more efficiently than a human driver could, thereby reducing fuel use. In the shorter term whilst vehicles are still reliant on internal combustion engines this is likely to hold true, particularly whilst there are opportunities for some lower level vehicle automation that can deliver these fuel efficiencies. For example, Bidoura Khondakar and Lina Kattan[30] showed that variable speed limit controls on vehicles could deliver fuel savings of up to 16%, with other studies proposing systems that might deliver even greater savings through optimizations.[31]

The longer term looks less certain from this perspective. Whilst automation may continue to deliver driver efficiencies, these benefits could be negated by the transition to battery electric vehicles (EVs), which is continuing at pace. Many existing and low-level CAVs are still reliant on petrol/diesel or hybrid engines. As newer models of CAV are developed, particularly within the private consumer market, it is inevitable that these will be dominated by EVs. Such efforts to replace petrol and diesel vehicles with electric (or hydrogen) vehicles will remove tailpipe emissions and—if the electricity or hydrogen is generated renewably—reduce the consumption of fossil fuels.

An area where benefits could be significant would be where shared mobility is adopted, particularly where this is coupled with vehicle electrification.[32] Shared mobility reduces the number of vehicles required and subsequently reduces resource demands for the production and maintenance of such vehicles. Research by Fagnant and Kockelman[33] concluded that, in a context where shared AVs made up just 3.5% of trips, one shared AV could replace approximately 12 privately owned vehicles. This emphasizes the significant potential value of a shared ownership model.

4.7 HEALTHY POPULATIONS

The need to reduce sedentary behaviours and improve the health of the population is a key challenge being grappled with at both national and local government levels. Active travel modes, which includes walking, cycling and other forms of active mobility, often are cited as ways to effectively deliver improvements in health whilst also alleviating other social (e.g., exclusion), environmental (e.g., pollution) and economic (e.g., congestion) challenges facing cities. The evidence is clear that the positive health benefits of increasing active travel far outweigh any negatives (e.g., risk from other road users or exposure to pollution).[34]

The impact of CAVs on population health is dependent on the extent of the uptake of them and in the specific types of vehicles where it happens. If private passenger services are the growth area, then CAVs will only serve to reinforce the sedentary behaviours that are so problematic at present. Evidence has highlighted how increasing vehicle-miles travelled through CAVs would likely lead to a decrease in active and public transport use.[35] If the growth of CAVs leans more towards shared or public transport, then the picture might look quite different.

The extent to which investments to enable a smoother integration of CAVs might be sought at the expense of investments in other modes is also potentially problematic. If investments that seek to support healthy populations, such as active travel infrastructure, decline in order to facilitate CAVs, then this could be damaging for efforts to increase population health. One interviewee, an advocate for more liveable urban environments, summarized it as follows:

> Increased deployment of CAVs would have implications on infrastructure and you'd have to make infrastructure changes as a result. Does that then come at the expense of the welcome increase in cycle infrastructure, the improvements to walking infrastructure that we've seen. So I think there is a risk that government accelerates the development of autonomous vehicles without full consideration of the potential for … unintended side effects. And even the potential for increased congestion … if you have that kind of world where … loads and loads of people making point to point journeys [by CAVs] that they would in the past have walked or cycled.

4.8 SUMMARY

In this chapter we have shed light on how CAVs could impact on other important agendas being pursued by local policymakers to help enhance the liveability of cities. Whilst CAVs are argued to present opportunities to improve safety, increase accessibility, reduce emissions and create new opportunities for work, they also pose risks to these agendas, and this has been demonstrated in the literature and through our interviews. Much of this relates to the extended transitional period over which CAVs might be deployed. There is a risk for conflict between road users during this period, and decisions made in the short-term might lead to path dependencies that problematize the pursuit of these concurrent agendas in the future.

NOTES

[1] Southworth M (2003) Measuring the liveable city. *Built Environment*, 29(4): 343–354. doi:10.2148/benv.29.4.343.54293.

[2] Kenworthy JR and Laube FB (1999) Patterns of automobile dependence in cities: An international overview of key physical and economic dimensions with some implications for urban policy. *Transportation Research Part A: Policy and Practice*, 33: 691–723. doi:10.1016/S0965-8564(99)00006-3.

[3] See https://www.who.int/news-room/fact-sheets/detail/road-traffic-injuries/.

[4] See https://www.brake.org.uk/get-involved/take-action/mybrake/knowledge-centre/uk-road-safety/.

[5] See https://www.gov.uk/government/news/the-highway-code-8-changes-you-need-to-know-from-29-january-2022/.

[6] McKinsey (2016) *Automotive Revolution—Perspective Towards 2030*. https://www.mckinsey.com/~/media/mckinsey/industries/automotive%20and%20assembly/our%20insights/disruptive%20trends%20that%20will%20transform%20the%20auto%20industry/auto%202030%20report%20

jan%202016.pdf; Arbib J and Seba T (2017) *Rethinking Transportation 2020–2030: Disruption of Transportation and the Collapse of the Internal-Combustion Vehicle & Oil Industries.* RethinkX. https://tonyseba.com/wp-content/uploads/2020/10/RethinkingTransportation_May_FINAL-LRR.pdf

[7] Mueller AS, Cicchino JB and Zuby DS (2020) *What Humanlike Errors Do Autonomous Vehicles Need to Avoid to Maximize Safety?* Arlington, VA: Insurance Institute for Highway Safety.

[8] Seraj M and Qiu TZ (2021) Multilane microscopic modeling to measure mobility and safety consequences of mixed traffic in freeway weaving sections. *Journal of Advanced Transportation*, 2021: art. 6639649. doi:10.1155/2021/6639649.

[9] Noy IY, Shinar D and Horrey WJ (2018) Automated driving: Safety blind spots. *Safety Science*, 102: 68–78. doi: 10.1016/j.ssci.2017.07.018.

[10] Hulse LM, Xie H and Galea ER (2018) Perceptions of autonomous vehicles: Relationships with road users, risk, gender and age. *Safety Science*, 102: 1–13. doi: 10.1016/j.ssci.2017.10.001.

[11] Millard-Ball A (2018) Pedestrians, autonomous vehicles, and cities. *Journal of Planning Education and Research*, 39(1): 6–12. doi: 10.1177/0739456X16675674.

[12] Choi JK and Ji YG (2015) Investigating the importance of trust on adopting an autonomous vehicle. *International Journal of Human–Computer Interaction*, 31: 692–702. Doi: 10.1080/10447318.2015.1070549.

[13] Razmi Rad S, Farah H, Taale H, van Arem B and Hoogendoorn SP (2020) Design and operation of dedicated lanes for connected and automated vehicles on motorways: A conceptual framework and research agenda. *Transportation Research Part C: Emerging Technologies*, 117: art. 102664. doi: 10.1016/j.trc.2020.102664.

[14] Millard-Ball (2018), see Reference 11.

[15] Hull A and O'Holleran C (2014) Bicycle infrastructure: Can good design encourage cycling? *Urban, Planning and Transport Research*, 2: 369–406. doi: 10.1080/21650020.2014.955210.

[16] Blau M, Akar G and Nasar J (2018) Driverless vehicles' potential influence on bicyclist facility preferences. *International Journal of Sustainable Transportation*, 12: 665–674. doi:10.1080/15568318.2018.1425781.

[17] Hamilton-Baillie B and Jones P (2005) Improving traffic behaviour and safety through urban design. *Proceedings of the Institution of Civil Engineers—Civil Engineering*, 158(5): 39–47. doi:10.1680/cien.2005.158.5.39.

[18] Faber K and van Lierop D (2020) How will older adults use automated vehicles? Assessing the role of AVs in overcoming perceived mobility barriers. *Transportation Research Part A: Policy and Practice*, 133: 353–363. doi: 10.1016/j.tra.2020.01.022.

[19] Li S, Blythe P, Zhang Y, Edwards S, Xing J, Guo W, Ji Y, Goodman P and Namdeo A (2021) Should older people be considered a homogeneous group when interacting with Level 3 automated vehicles? *Transportation Research Part F: Traffic Psychology and Behaviour*, 78: 446–465. doi:10.1016/j.trf.2021.03.004.

[20] Claypool H, Bin-Nun A and Gerlach J (2017) *Self-Driving Cars: The Impact on People with Disabilities.* Boston, MA: Ruderman Family Foundation.

[21] Crisp R, Ferrari E, Gore T, Green S, McCarthy, Rae A, Reeve K and Stevens M (2018) *Tackling Transport-Related Barriers to Employment in Low-Income Neighbourhoods.* York, UK: Joseph Rowntree Foundation.

[22] Bissell D, Birtchnell T, Elliott A and Hsu EL (2020) Autonomous automobilities: The social impacts of driverless vehicles. *Current Sociology*, 68(1): 116–134, at 123. doi:10.1177/0011392118816743.

[23] Duarte F and Ratti C (2018) The Impact of Autonomous Vehicles on Cities: A Review. *Journal of Urban Technology*, 25: 3–18, at 10. doi:10.1080/10630732.2018.1493883.

[24] See https://www.forbes.com/sites/carltonreid/2021/11/06/bidens-12-trillion-infrastructure-bill-hastens-beacon-wearing-for-bicyclists-and-pedestrians-to-enable-detection-by-connected-cars/?sh=4480a36a5a3d/.

[25] Reid C (2021, November 6) Biden's $1.2 trillion infrastructure bill hastens beacons for bicyclists and pedestrians enabling detection by connected cars. *Forbes*. https://www.forbes.com/sites/carlton-reid/2021/11/06/bidens-12-trillion-infrastructure-bill-hastens-beacon-wearing-for-bicyclists-and-pedestrians-to-enable-detection-by-connected-cars/?sh=57c535115a3d

[26] Berge SH, Hagenzieker M, Farah H and de Winter J (2022) Do cyclists need HMIs in future automated traffic? An interview study. *Transportation Research Part F: Traffic Psychology and Behaviour*, 84: 33–52. doi:10.1016/j.trf.2021.11.013.

[27] Taeihagh A and Lim HSM (2019) Governing autonomous vehicles: Emerging responses for safety, liability, privacy, cybersecurity, and industry risks. *Transport Reviews*, 39: 103–128. doi:10.1080/01441647.2018.1494640.

[28] Beede DN, Powers R and Ingram C (2017) The employment impact of autonomous vehicles. *SSRN Scholarly Paper No. ID 3022818, Social Science Research Network*. doi:10.2139/ssrn.3022818.

[29] Bissell et al. (2020), see Reference 22.

[30] Khondaker B and Kattan L (2015) Variable speed limit: A microscopic analysis in a connected vehicle environment. *Transportation Research Part C: Emerging Technologies*, 58: 146–159. doi:10.1016/j.trc.2015.07.014.

[31] Milakis D, van Arem B and van Wee B (2017) Policy and society related implications of automated driving: A review of literature and directions for future research. *Journal of Intelligent Transportation Systems*, 21(4): 324–348. doi:10.1080/15472450.2017.1291351.

[32] Shaheen S and Bouzaghrane MA (2019) Mobility and energy impacts of shared automated vehicles: A review of recent literature. *Current Sustainable/Renewable Energy Reports*, 6: 193–200. doi:10.1007/s40518-019-00135-2.

[33] Fagnant DJ and Kockelman K (2015) Preparing a nation for autonomous vehicles: Opportunities, barriers and policy recommendations. *Transportation Research Part A: Policy and Practice*, 77: 167–181. doi:10.1016/j.tra.2015.04.003.

[34] Mueller N, Rojas-Rueda D, Cole-Hunter T, de Nazelle A, Dons E, Gerike R, Götschi T, Int Panis L, Kahlmeier S and Nieuwenhuijsen M (2015) Health impact assessment of active transportation: A systematic review. *Preventive Medicine*, 76: 103–114. doi:10.1016/j.ypmed.2015.04.010.

[35] Soteropoulos A, Berger M and Ciari F (2019) Impacts of automated vehicles on travel behaviour and land use: An international review of modelling studies. *Transport Reviews*, 39: 29–49. doi:10.1080/01441647.2018.1523253.

5. RESPONDING TO THE ARRIVAL OF INCREASINGLY CONNECTED AND AUTONOMOUS VEHICLES

Keywords: regulation; built environment; public acceptance; guidance

5.1 INTRODUCTION

The impending arrival of increasingly connected and autonomous vehicles (CAVs) on public roads will have wide ranging impacts on society. The highly disruptive potential of CAVs on the existing transport system and wider built environment has been outlined in the preceding chapters of this book.

In this chapter, we turn our attention to the abilities of policymakers at different levels of government to respond to these challenges. This addresses the final two questions of the Policy Expo:

- What do best-practice policy solutions look like, and how can local and regional policymakers plan proactively?

- What do national policymakers and infrastructure providers need to do? And what must be resolved locally?

In tackling these final questions, this chapter explores several different issues, including: the role of the regulatory environment and how local policymakers feature in this; the availability and use of guidance and best practice; the priorities for preparing the built environment; and the role of public engagement as part of this response.

5.2 ESTABLISHING A REGULATORY ENVIRONMENT

As the technology that underpins more highly automated vehicles advances, the need to develop an effective regulatory environment becomes ever more pressing. So far policymakers and other industry actors have largely avoided responding with any decisiveness to the question of how highly automated vehicle should be regulated.[1] This reflects the highly complex challenge of doing so, bearing in mind the far-reaching impacts that CAVs will potentially have on multiple aspects of social, economic and cultural life, and the concomitant need for regulation to address the complex interactions between them and the technology. However, increasingly regulation is under discussion and scrutiny.

5.2.1 National level

It is at the national level where, for most countries, the responsibility and power to develop the relevant regulatory frameworks lie. One source of insight into the status of the strengths of different regulatory environments across countries is the KPMG Autonomous Vehicles Readiness Index (AVRI).[2] Whilst the index does have some limitations, which were discussed in previous chapters, the KPMG report does nevertheless highlight that it is only comparatively

Regional Studies Policy Impact Books
© 2022 Stephen Parkes and Ed Ferrari

https://doi.org/10.1080/2578711X.2022.2085929

recently—in the last two or three years—that national governments have started to act in earnest on the question of regulation.

Even in countries with a comparatively mature discussion on CAV regulation, there is an important distinction to be drawn between an emerging regulatory environment which is supportive of the technology and its diffusion, on the one hand, and one that focuses more on restricting the development or adoption of CAVs, or at least certain aspects or use cases. With this distinction in mind, it is notable that the KPMG index ranks more highly those countries where regulations are already in place and the resultant regulatory environment is supportive of CAVs and concomitantly places few restrictions on their development or adoption. So, the strength of the regulatory environment in this regard is the extent to which the regulatory environment is conducive to CAVs rather than restrictive. In the latest version of the KPMG index,[3] the highest scoring countries included Australia, Finland, Singapore and the Netherlands. The lowest scoring countries included India, Mexico and Brazil. The contrast of Global North and Global South countries here is telling of the differences in preparedness seen nationally, but may also reflect a normative conception of the economic and social role of CAVs and how they may best serve established trajectories in the development of built environment, infrastructure and levels of automobility.

Australia is one of the early movers on AV regulation, and much of this is being undertaken through the National Transport Commission's Automated Vehicle Program.[4] This initiative is seeking an "end-to-end" regulatory approach that can support CAVs at all levels of automation being deployed safely and commercially.[5] Spain is another country where, in 2020, the national government sought to enact changes to the legal environment to help accommodate CAVs.

In the UK, there have been recent developments in the form of the publishing of the long-awaited Law Commission's joint report on *Autonomous Vehicles*.[6] This report was the result of a three-stage consultation process that began in late 2018. An initial consultation on safety assurance and legal liability was following by a second consultation (in October 2020) specifically looking at the role of CAVs in public transport. The third and final consultation as part of this process sought to consolidate the collected evidence and develop overarching proposals for next steps in the regulation of CAVs in the UK.

One outcome of the Law Commission's work has been a recommendation of changes to how driver responsibility is acknowledged in an automated vehicle. This proposal has significant implications with regards to liability and seeks to distinguish between "self-driving" and "driver assisted" cases (Box 5.1).

5.2.2 Cities and regions

If the progress on the development of national regulatory frameworks has been only relatively recent, the development and implementation of regulations at more localized levels has

> **Box 5.1: User-in-charge**
>
> **User-in-charge:** Once a vehicle meets the threshold of being "self-driving" or fully autonomous, the person in the driving seat should be regarded as a "user-in-charge" rather than a driver. This is a profound change and would mean that the user could not be prosecuted for driving offences that arise from the driving task. This would include dangerous driving, exceeding the speed limit or passing through a red light. The user would still be responsible for other driver duties such as ensuring passengers have seatbelts fastened.
>
> *Source*: Law Commission *Autonomous Vehicles*[29]

received even more limited attention to date. In part this may reflect an endogenous focus on the vehicle, its capabilities, and its ontological and operational relationships with other vehicles and human operators. These traditionally form the scope of well-established national and supranational legal frameworks, such as on vehicle homologation, which now need to be extended into the automated domain. To take an example, the United Nations Economic Commission for Europe's (UNECE) work on shaping the legal framework for intelligent transport systems, including vehicle automation, focuses principally on vehicular systems and interoperability across national borders.[7] Yet a fully developed regulatory framework that properly seeks to balance the benefits and potential negative impacts of CAVs will necessarily bring into focus local regulation, especially as they relate to the use of infrastructure, the built environment and place-based variation in the relationships—formal or implied—between vehicular traffic and other road users. Part of the challenge is that the powers and tools available to policymakers can be highly variable, reflecting differentials in the degree of centralization or local devolution that might exist across jurisdictions.

The extent to which city and regional policymakers are empowered to make decisions and are able to establish and shape their local regulatory environment is an important factor in determining how they may respond to CAVs. In this section we highlight some examples of the extent to which local policymakers are incorporated into decision-making and the challenges that emerge from balancing competing influences.

In the United States, the Automated Vehicles Comprehensive Plan,[8] published in 2021, sets out to promote collaboration, modernize the regulatory environment and help prepare the wider transport system for more highly automated vehicles. Again, however, the regulatory dimension to this is largely related to the regulation of vehicle designs and features. The state level is where further powers can be enacted. As of 2018, 35 US states had legislated for or issued executive orders relating to CAVs. Cities themselves can also intervene with regards to how streets and urban environments operate and the transit services within them.[9] In a recent study examining US city preparedness for AVs, Yonah Freemark and colleagues[10] discovered that cities feared the influence of state legislatures around CAVs and how a lack of certainty prohibited effective and timely policymaking around AVs:

> Several cities expressed concern about the role of higher levels of government. The spectre of pre-emption may limit or delay local AV policymaking; a clearer division of responsibilities among different levels of government combined with state authorization for using municipal powers to help shape the arrival of AVs might help to alleviate such hesitation.

This potential conflict between state and city governments and how it might influence outcomes was highlighted by one of the Expo's participants, an academic with specific knowledge of the US context:

> Some states here [in the United States], Texas is one of them and maybe Arizona as well, [are] trying to pre-empt local regulations of AVs. Like the state just says you on the local level cannot regulate AVs. And that's part of creating a favourable environment [for AVs] because the vehicles are assured that they can use the roadways as the state government sees fit, which is different than what a city would do.

In the UK, the trialling of more highly automated vehicles is possible on any UK road without the requirement for additional permits, providing current vehicle and traffic laws are complied with. The UK government's code of conduct on trialling CAVs does stipulate that an organization looking to trial such vehicles must have a driver or external operator who can take control of the vehicle if needed, the vehicle must be roadworthy and insured.[11] Beyond that, there are minimal rules governing the testing of CAVs and local authorities have few if any powers to influence whether and how CAVs are trialled in their area.

Despite this, however, there is often significant engagement in practice between local policymakers and organizations seeking to run trials in the UK. This is something the code of conduct also advises, specifically that "those planning tests should speak with the road and enforcement authorities, develop engagement plans, and have data recorders fitted".[12]

The UK situation may be contrasted with that in China, where individual cities have more control over how CAVs are being trialled and deployed and may decide whether to legislate to allow automated vehicles to be trialled. For instance, Beijing was the first Chinese city to allow testing on public roads.[13] This was the result of collaboration between the city's transport commission, traffic management bureau, and the economy and information technology commission. The regulations developed in Beijing have become a model for other Chinese cities.

5.2.3 Key regulatory considerations for local policymakers

The extent to which regulatory tools are available to local policymakers is very much dependent on the national context. It remains an evolving area of policy and varies from country to country.

In the previous two chapters we outlined some of the key challenges facing local policymakers with regards to the arrival of increasingly highly automated vehicles. These challenges are partly associated with the uncertainties that CAVs bring for the built environment. They arise, for instance, from the extended time horizons over which CAVs will be deployed, different ownership scenarios and what role CAVs might fulfil, and the impacts they will have on transport networks and wider spatial structures. They are also associated with the risks that CAVs might pose to concurrent policy agendas that are being pursued seeking to enhance the liveability of cities—which is a key objective for many local policymakers. This includes agendas on safety, accessibility, access to employment, protection of the environment and enhancement of public health.

Whilst much of the regulation is being developed at national or, in some cases, state level, and there is a concern over how local policymakers can influence this, it is also vital that cities and regions have the tools and skills available locally to help them influence the CAV agenda to protect their own interests. Evidence from the United States, for example, suggests that cities do not feel well equipped with the tools to manage these pressures at present.

Despite the primacy of national regulation, cities and other localities do provide the basic frameworks within which urban functions are managed, such as spatial planning and urban design.[14] This is important because it means local policymakers, and through governance structures local citizens, may have some ability to shape how the built environment responds to the increasing presence of CAVs. As discussed in the preceding chapter, a proactive stance on preparing the built environment for the arrival of CAVs could yield important outcomes in terms of securing the most positive and widespread benefits for local places and their populations. It should also not be forgotten that, beyond the regulation of CAVs specifically, local jurisdictions may be able to exert degrees of regulatory control and influence in other, related ways. For example, the arrival of ridesharing platforms such as Uber and /Lyft, dockless bike sharing and electric scooter schemes has forced local policymakers to respond to these disruptive technologies, and they are often equipped with local policy tools—for example, licensing—that can help them influence how these services and developments unfold. Given that the future of ridesharing and increased vehicular automation are closely conjoined, this does raise the prospect that a wider set of tools in the urban governance arsenal can be pressed into the service of influencing CAV roll-out, even if the regulatory framework for vehicle automation is otherwise largely centralized and permissive.

Beyond seeking to regulate or influence the arrival of CAVs, local areas can take on other important new roles. The critical role that city governments and local authorities play in creating and maintaining key datasets—for example, on cadastres, land-use mapping, signage, land use, and infrastructure availability and restrictions—means that cities could find themselves taking on new roles as "mediators and data catalysts".[15]

https://doi.org/10.1080/2578711X.2022.2085929

For local policymakers to be able to effectively manage the arrival of more highly CAVs and the pressures they bring, there are some key areas of regulation that will need to be considered:

- **Road pricing, congestion charging and tolling** can be used to incentivize or disincentivize the use of particular vehicles types in time and space. Pricing schemes could cover degrees of automation in combination with other vehicle characteristics (e.g., size, noise and emissions).

- **Selective lane and turn restrictions**, which could be used to constrain CAVs to, or prohibit CAVs from, specific routes or zones—for example, school streets during certain times of the day.

- The **creation, maintenance and use of data assets**, such as geofences and mapping data, may inform the way that vehicle decision-making algorithms work. Through controlling data, local authorities could enforce vehicle behaviour dynamically, for example, to disperse traffic away from congested areas or make space for emergency vehicles.

- **Parking regulations** may be important in incentivizing the relationship between CAVs and the kerbside, and may be of particular value in promoting shared vehicle use in dense urban environments.

- **Kerbside pricing**, including for CAV loading and drop-off, may help to manage kerbside demand,

- **Electric vehicle (EV) charging infrastructure** may—for a limited time while vehicle drivetrain technology matures—be a useful mechanism through which to encourage or dissuade stationary CAVs, given that most will also be EVs.

- **Workplace levies or taxes**, integrated into local business tax regimes, could be used to influence the use of CAVs for private commuting.

- **Licensing**, for example, for taxis, ride-sharing and public transport vehicles, is a local regulatory mechanism that may also help to influence how and when CAVs of different types are used.

- **Planning rules and design codes** for new buildings could reduce parking requirements, discourage multiple vehicles ownership or single-occupancy vehicle use, and promote shared CAV models in new residential developments.

- Wider **spatial planning policies and land-use regulation**—aimed at influencing urban spatial structure over the longer term through policies governing the location and density of housing and employment areas—could help to influence the economic trade-offs implied in CAV ownership and use.

5.3 GUIDANCE AND LEARNING THROUGH BEST PRACTICE

The growing attention on CAVs and the impending arrival of more highly automated vehicles on public roads has prompted the development of guidance and the sharing of best practice. This guidance is often developed at the national level by governments or transport bodies to be accessed by those operating in the field. There is also the accumulated knowledge and insights that are shared across local government and related non-governmental bodies, through both informal and formal networks.

Across countries, variations in the existing legal and regulatory structures, the institutions that exist and the strength of these, and a range of other place specific factors (e.g., existing land-use and transport trends) means that what works in one country may not work elsewhere. Whilst it is beyond the scope of this book to examine the extent of guidance across all countries, some examples can be discussed to highlight how guidance has been developed.

At a supranational level, the European Commission has undertaken a range of activities around CAVs, recognizing the potential impact on European roads and the highly integrated nature of these road networks across country boundaries. Work undertaken or commissioned includes a 2018 "communication" outlining the European Union's (EU) strategy on connected and automated mobility in Europe.[16] This document sought to unite a path for EU members, industry and other partners to work together. The aim of this, as the document describes, was so that the " EU seizes the opportunities offered by driverless mobility, while anticipating and mitigating new challenges for society".

Some of the steps taken by the European Commission have been the development of further guidance, including recommendations on CAV ethics,[17] and guidance on the assessment and categorization of CAVs.[18] For the European Commission, these efforts are to ensure consistency across member states.

In Canada, the development of a CAV "Policy Framework"[19] for the country has sought to ensure that CAVs are operated safely in the built environment. This framework established safe testing guidance to trialling organizations and the jurisdictions where such trials might take place; attempted to align key policies and legal considerations across the Canadian jurisdictions; and extended partnerships across government, industry and academia.

Other organizations and academics are also developing guidance. For instance, RAND—the global policy think tank—has published guidance for policymakers.[20] The RAND guidance is wide-ranging and notably includes guidance for policymakers that extends to risks around market failure, regulation and liability. Insights have also been provided from early adopting cities and regions in the United States.[21]

The CAV market is sufficiently developed that guidance is increasingly available. At supranational and national levels policymakers are seeking to shape the agenda through this guidance. More targeted and localized guidance is also available, building from lessons gathered through trials and early adopting locations. However, none of the guidance is particularly consistent and needs to account for context-specific factors in each country or location. Our interviews explored how best-practice guidance is, or should be, shared. One interviewee, with expertise in running CAV trials, summarized the importance of clear and accessible guidance for time- and resource-restricted local policymakers.

> I think there are a few [barriers to engaging with best practice guidance]. One is the time and resource availability to fully consider twenty different sources of information to try and understand which one is the best. There's the simplification of where they access information and the quality of it, that I think is important. It needs to be really simple for them, it also needs to be available from a single location. They need to have access to it readily and it needs to convey to them in their own language what they can and should do and what they can't do and should avoid. It needs to be very simple and accessible. I also think it needs to sit in a way that it's a living document.

The lessons that are increasingly available from testbed locations or early adopters offer important insights for policymakers who are later adopters to CAVs or lack the resources to undertaken extensive planning around them. Learning from elsewhere remains common in modern transport planning and practice.[22] Policy transfer underpins how knowledge and best practice is shared and adopted.

There is evidence of how knowledge transfer is taking place around CAVs and how this helps local policymakers to effectively plan for them. One dimension of this is through the trialling of AVs, which is often undertaken by consortiums of organizations bringing different skills and knowledge. For example, in Box 5.2 we feature a case study of Project Endeavour in the UK. This project included partners such as Oxbotica (AV software), DG Cities (integration of smart city technologies), TRL (safety and compliance expertise), BSI (business improvement) and Oxfordshire County Council.

Beyond specific projects or trials, knowledge transfer is also taking place between universities and firms. For example, Aston University in the UK has established a knowledge transfer partnership with the AV company Aurrigo to help develop systems to improve vehicle safety.[23] Such partnerships, whether formal or informal, were also cited by interviewees participating in this Policy Expo. For local governments that lack specific expertise or capacity around CAVs, such partnerships offer valuable ways to increase capacity to develop plans and organizations knowledge.

5.4 THE BUILT ENVIRONMENT

The rapid uptake of the private car as a means of transportation in the mid-20th century led to a redesign of cities to better accommodate this form of travel. Road networks were widened and straightened, and ultimately designed more with the vehicle in mind.[24] There is a question mark now over the extent to which cities will redesign themselves for the benefit of CAVs.

Box 5.2: Case study: Creating safe CAV services
Findings from Project Endeavour in the UK

Background

Running from March 2019 to autumn 2021, Project Endeavour was established with the goal of increasing and upscaling the adoption of self-driving vehicles in the UK. This was led by Oxbotica and involved collaboration with DG Cities, Oxfordshire County Council, Immense, TRL and BSI. It builds on previous work in the same subject area by MERGE Greenwich. The ultimate goal of the project was to expand on previous work in this study area by

providing the chance for members of the public to experience the technology of AVs first-hand using live trials and demonstrations of the technology.

Four trials of AVs were delivered by the consortium: two in Oxford and one each in Birmingham and Greenwich (London). In terms of scale, the trials started with stakeholders to iron out any issues with the technology before being upscaled to include and engage the general public. The trials were publicized across a broad range of media channels, including printed leaflets and social media, to broaden the potential audience. In addition, a virtual reality relay of the Oxford trial was made available online to engage more people.

To gather insights into the impact of the trials, the project used the following methodology:

- Online survey distributed on social media exploring issues such as perception of the technology, interest in trying it and of using it in the future, as well as general travel attitudes.
- Pre- and post-trial surveys focusing on perceptions, experience and how participating in the trial had affected these positively or negatively.
- Post-trial interviews and online focus groups.

These were all analysed and incorporated into the findings in the report. The live trials included a short trip in an AV along with a human driver to take control if needed along a short route, whilst the virtual reality element comprised a video showcasing current AV technology and another presenting future potential of the technology.

The findings from the study suggested that whilst the technology was generally regarded as safe, the presence of a human driver to take control was important for some. Others

saw the potential for the technology to be safer because it removed the risk of human error. The study suggested that trust in the automation dropped when more complex obstacles, such as junctions, were approached. It was felt that more testing should be done before they are allowed on the road in public and safety features (such as an emergency stop button) were welcome, but that consideration of the needs to people with physical disabilities was needed in the design of the vehicles.

The Endeavour Project showed that perception of the safety of AVs tends to become more negative in line with the increase in the age of the participants. The results of the Greenwich trial found a 15% improvement in positive perception of the technology after participants had encountered the technology first hand. The study shows that the majority of the population is still unsure as to the safety of self-driving vehicles; however, the aforementioned 15% increase in improved perceptions from participants in live trials of the technology seems to indicate that such perceptions could be down to lack of contact with or understanding of it. The acceptance of AVs also intersects according to age, with 21% of over 55s feeling confident using an AV tomorrow compared with 35% for those aged 18–35. There is also a difference by gender, although this is not as clear cut, with 17% of female participants as opposed to 25% of male participants strongly agreeing that AVs will be trustworthy. The national survey also highlighted how over one-quarter of people are still undecided about AVs, with safety being the main issue, particularly on roads where AVs will be merging with human drivers.

In conclusion, the study highlighted how there is still a long way to go to convince the majority of the public as to the safety of AVs, although this may be down simply to lack of awareness and understanding of it. The hugely positive increase in trust in the technology after participants have undertaken the in-person trials make a strong case for more public engagement of this kind to be carried out to build public confidence, particularly amongst participants aged 55+ given the lower levels of confidence this age group demonstrated in the technology.

Source: Case study produced using evidence published by the Endeavour Project[30]

There are views on both sides of this argument, and this is something that was evident in our interviews. For the majority of places, the indication is that there is limited work being undertaken to prepare the environment specifically for CAVs.[25] With questions still outstanding about how CAVs ultimately will shape the built environment, there is likely to be a reluctance to spend already constrained resources on extensive planning efforts.

The extent to which a city responds to CAVs is likely to be motivated by a broad range of factors, including their existing transport system and trends, but also what the political appetite is for such technology. We have explored already (see section 4.3) about how there is concern that CAVs might lead to the need for more segregation of users, a reminder of planning trends of the mid-20th century. This raises important questions around the prioritization of road space for different users; car-friendly cities will likely reinforce these trends through accommodation of CAVs.

One further dimension of the actions needed around infrastructure and the built environment is around data. CAVs themselves form a data platform with huge amounts of data being collected by and shared between vehicles.[26] Cities are also emerging as anchor points in complex partnerships between different public and private agencies. In this role, they collect data on transport patterns and behaviours, but also have a responsibility for cybersecurity and privacy. There is also an important role in drawing together and providing access to data that are vital for the safe operation of CAVs, including traffic lights, crossing points, road dimensions and location of curbs, street lighting, and traffic flows. The ability to compile and easily transmit this type of data will require substantial financial investment for many cities, and it is not clear where such financial support will come from.[27]

In addition, many cities already outlay significant costs to maintain road surfaces, markings and signs. Maintenance and enhancements of this existing infrastructure will also be important for CAVs. Much of the dialogue around CAVs and their benefits allude to a significant redesign of spatial structures. This might include a reduction in parking allocations, particularly in city centres or the need to increase drop-off points as passengers alight from their automated vehicle. In addition, any responses around CAVs will be foreshadowed by the need to deliver widespread EV charging infrastructure, which is a priority for many cities at present.

5.5 ENGAGING THE PUBLIC

Public acceptance will be critical to the widespread adoption of CAVs and is therefore a key part of the response to the arrival of increasingly AVs. Whilst the responsibility of communicating the potential impacts of CAVs is not solely that of local policymakers (national government and industry are also vital in this), it is an important consideration and potential challenge. Whilst much of the debate around CAVs has centred on when they might see full-scale uptake, the type of ownership models that might emerge, and the impacts on spatial patterns in cities

https://doi.org/10.1080/2578711X.2022.2085929

and traffic levels, there has been only limited debate at the *public* level over the role of CAVs in future transport systems.

This may in part be due to the longer term and uncertain time horizons over which CAVs are emerging. Certainly, the most transformative aspects of CAVs, for example, high levels of automation with minimal/no requirements for drivers to intervene, will take years to be fully established. Therefore, it is difficult to explore public acceptance when we are not sure exactly what things will look like.

A range of studies have been conducted to explore public acceptance. This includes academic research through surveys and in driving simulators but also in real-world test environments. Much of the work around acceptance is linked to perceptions of safety.

One of the key pro-CAV arguments is that it will improve safety for all road users. There remains much to do in terms of proving, beyond doubt, that CAVs are infallible in this regard, however, and indeed they may never reach that point. For now, this means there remains a question mark over safety in and around such vehicles and this damages public acceptance. Some studies suggest that the safety benefits of CAVs are well understood and seen as a "selling point" for potential users. In contrast, other studies have suggested that concerns over safety are one of the overriding issues. Work undertaken in La Rochelle, France, evaluating AV demonstrations in the city[28] showed that whilst surveyed residents were generally supportive of AVs, including buses and cars, only a quarter felt that AVs would be safer than human-driven vehicles.

To explore further how trials are undertaken and what impact these might have on the public, and levels of acceptance, we have included a case study box of the Endeavour Project, which ran between 2019 and 2021 in the UK.

The relationship between CAVs and the promotion of liveable cities can also be interwoven with how we interact with, and feel about, the places we travel through, and how CAVs impact on these. One submission to our Policy Expo summarized this as follows:

> CAVs are not simply a means of transportation but can also be viewed as an object, operated by non-human means, which intrudes into the places where we live and work. These CAVs "coming into" our neighbourhoods include not only cars and buses but potentially also automated grocery and delivery vehicles. Whether individuals are comfortable with CAVs entering these spaces, and whether they trust or [should] "trust" those vehicles, is potentially dependent upon how they view a particular place, and how that place is being used.

This highlights how important it is to think about the non-utilitarian impacts of CAVs, which are often omitted from the discourse around this topic. It also serves to demonstrate the unintended consequences of this disruptive technology.

5.6 SUMMARY

Responding to an increasing presence of CAVs will require wide-ranging actions delivered by supra-national, national and local decision-makers. In this chapter we have explored how the regulatory environment is being developed and some of the conflicts that might emerge between different levels of government. Guidance and best practice remain nascent and largely only informally shared; more consistent and accessible information will broaden the extent to which later adopting cities can engage with these issues. The built environment will likely be transformed in response to an increasing presence of CAVs, but this is costly and dependent on many place-based factors. Finally, public engagement is well underway, as highlighted by the Project Endeavour case study, through arguably there remains much to do and a wider public debate about the role and impacts of CAVs is an essential step.

NOTES

[1] Mordue G, Yeung A and Wu F (2020) The looming challenges of regulating high level autonomous vehicles. *Transportation Research Part A: Policy and Practice*, 132, 174–187. doi:10.1016/j.tra.2019.11.007.

[2] KPMG (2020) *2020 Autonomous Vehicles Readiness Index.* https://home.kpmg/xx/en/home/insights/2020/06/autonomous-vehicles-readiness-index.html

[3] The year 2020 at the time of writing.

[4] See https://www.ntc.gov.au/transport-reform/automated-vehicle-program/.

[5] National Transport Commission (2020) *Automated Vehicle Program Approach.* https://www.ntc.gov.au/sites/default/files/assets/files/Automated%20vehicle%20approach.pdf.

[6] See https://www.lawcom.gov.uk/project/automated-vehicles/.

[7] UNECE Inland Transport Committee (2020) *World Forum for Harmonization of Vehicle Regulations: Framework Document on Automated/Autonomous Vehicles.* Geneva: UNECE Inland Transport Committee. https://unece.org/automated-driving/.

[8] USDOT (2021) *Automated Vehicles Comprehensive Plan.* US Department of Transportation (USDOT). https://www.transportation.gov/sites/dot.gov/files/2021-01/USDOT_AVCP.pdf.

[9] Freemark Y, Hudson A and Zhao J (2019) Are cities prepared for autonomous vehicles? *Journal of the American Planning Association*, 85(2): 133–151. doi:10.1080/01944363.2019.1603760.

[10] Freemark et al. (2019), see Reference 9, at 148.

[11] See https://www.gov.uk/government/publications/trialling-automated-vehicle-technologies-in-public/code-of-practice-automated-vehicle-trialling#general-requirements/.

[12] In the UK, excepting major strategic roads such as motorways, local highway authorities have statutory responsibility for operating, administering and maintaining public roads.

[13] KPMG (2020), see Reference 2.

[14] Aoyama Y and Alvarez Leon LF (2021) Urban governance and autonomous vehicles. *Cities*, 119: art. 103410. doi:10.1016/j.cities.2021.103410.

[15] Aoyama and Alvarez Leon (2021), see Reference 14.

[16] Communication from the Commission to the European Parliament, the Council, the European Economic and Social Committee, the Committee of the Regions (2018) *On the Road to Automated Mobility: An EU Strategy for Mobility of the Future.* https://eur-lex.europa.eu/legal-content/EN/TXT/PDF/?uri=CELEX:52018DC0283&from=EN

[17] European Commission (2020) *Ethics of Connected and Automated Vehicles: Recommendations on Road Safety, Privacy, Fairness, Explainability and Responsibility.* doi:10.2777/966923; https://op.europa.eu/en/publication-detail/-/publication/89624e2c-f98c-11ea-b44f-01aa75ed71a1/language-en/.

[18] European Commission (2019) *Guidelines on the Exemption Procedure for the EU Approval of Automated Vehicles.* https://ec.europa.eu/docsroom/documents/34802

[19] PPSC Working Group on Automated and Connected Vehicles (2019) *Automated and Connected Vehicles Policy Framework for Canada.* https://www.comt.ca/Reports/AVCV%20Policy%20Framework%202019.pdf/.

[20] RAND (2016) *Autonomous Vehicle Technology: A Guide for Policymakers.* https://www.rand.org/content/dam/rand/pubs/research_reports/RR400/RR443-2/RAND_RR443-2.pdf/.

[21] Chatman DG and Moran ME (2019) *Insights on Autonomous Vehicle Policy from Early Adopter Cities and Regions.* Berkeley: Institute of Transportation Studies, University of California. https://escholarship.org/uc/item/4xv6z4mj

[22] Glaser M, Bertolini L, te Brömmelstroet M, Blake O and Ellingson C (2021) Learning through policy transfer? Reviewing a decade of scholarship for the field of transport. *Transport Reviews*, 1–19. doi:10.1080/01441647.2021.2003472.

[23] See https://www.aston.ac.uk/latest-news/aston-university-and-aurrigo-use-knowledge-transfer-partnership-make-autonomous/

[24] Duarte F and Ratti C (2018) The impact of autonomous vehicles on cities: A review. *Journal of Urban Technology*, 25: 3–18. doi:10.1080/10630732.2018.1493883.

[25] Freemark et al. (2019), see Reference 10.

[26] Duarte and Ratti (2018), see Reference 24.

[27] Aoyama and Alvarez Leon (2021) , see Reference 14.

[28] Piao J, McDonald M, Hounsell N, Graindorge M, Graindorge T and Malhene N (2016) Public views towards implementation of automated vehicles in urban areas. *Transportation Research Procedia*, 14: 2168–2177. doi:10.1016/j.trpro.2016.05.232.

[29] See https://www.lawcom.gov.uk/project/automated-vehicles/.

[30] DG Cities (2021) *Creating Safe Self-Driving Services: Findings from Project Endeavour.* https://tinyurl.com/2ymja5wp/.

6. CONCLUSIONS

Keywords: CAVs, transitions, policy-making

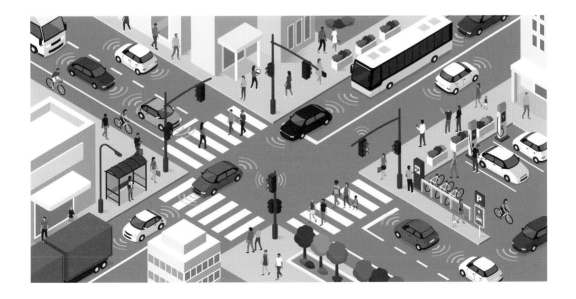

The development of connected and automated vehicles (CAVs) presents a significant challenge to local policymakers navigating a range of important policy issues and agendas. Connected vehicles are very much here, and more highly automated vehicles are on their way. How the transition to a world where there is a critical mass of autonomous vehicles (AVs) plays out remains very much uncertain, however.

6.1 AN UNCERTAIN FUTURE

CAVs do not simply represent a like-for-like replacement of non-CAVs. Their arrival will signify the potential for a fundamental shift in how urban environments are navigated, how goods are moved and how services are provided. In observing the development of CAVs, the attention of commentators naturally gravitates towards private passenger vehicles, and indeed it is likely that the most significant impacts on society and places will be felt if uptake amongst this part of the vehicle fleet is widespread. However, as we have outlined in this book, the automation of vehicles also reaches across freight, home deliveries, public transport, campus transport, etc., and it is vital that these are considered as part of the planning process. It is in these arenas—particularly the development of shared AVs that complement other transport modes—where we might expect the most tangible change in the near future.

Some of the overarching challenges facing policymakers, both nationally and locally, centre on the uncertainty over what time periods the different levels of automation may appear on public roads, and ultimately what level of automation is achievable. Optimistic assessments suggest that by the end of this decade we will see widespread deployment of advanced levels of automation in vehicles operating on public roads. More conservative—and perhaps realistic—views see this taking much longer. Regardless, CAVs represent a highly disruptive innovation.

The type of impact CAVs will have depends on the ownership models that emerge. For several years, shared mobility (for instance, conceptualized through Mobility as a Service—MaaS) has been presented as one of the solutions to problems facing the transport system. In such a scenario, users share access to vehicles, booking them when they are needed rather than owning them outright. If an arrival of more highly automated vehicles is coupled with an even greater shift towards shared mobility, then the consensus amongst our interviewees and the literature is that CAVs have the potential to make a positive contribution to future transport systems.

The alternative scenario is a model that would reinforce the widespread private car dependencies that have been the norm across the world for many decades. Under such a model,

https://doi.org/10.1080/2578711X.2022.2085930
© 2022 Stephen Parkes and Ed Ferrari

concurrent efforts by policymakers to deliver necessary enhancements to the liveability of urban environments are likely to be compromised. Even if the ultimate outcome is a hybrid between these two scenarios, it is vital that local policymakers have the appropriate powers, resources and skills to manage the impact of a widespread deployment of CAVs.

In this book we have also highlighted how the preparedness of communities for CAVs is variable. Predominantly, although not exclusively, it is countries in the Global North that are leading the way with taking steps to develop environments that are more conducive to CAVs. For example, in investing in the supporting digital infrastructure or developing regulations to account for the increasing automation of driver tasks in vehicles. But preparing for CAVs by paving the way for their growth is not the same thing as anticipating their myriad impacts and shaping that growth. Where countries are investing time and resources into preparing for CAVs, inevitably this trickles down to the urban level with cities and regions forming the testbed locations for resulting vehicle trials. It is important that later adopting countries, particularly those in the Global South, are not excluded from the dialogue happening currently around CAVs. The case study prepared by Dr Aliyu Kawu (see Box 2.1 in chapter 2) demonstrated how policymakers in Nigeria are grappling with even greater barriers to the deployment of CAVs, but this does not mean they should be excluded from the conversation.

Our Policy Expo has shed light on the realities of a transition to CAVs and why it is important to begin thinking about and planning for them now, rather than delaying. For cities and regions to tie in their existing planning goals with the advent of CAVs has been described as a "fleeting opportunity".[1] There are of course barriers to this. One overriding difficulty is the lack of clarity over where responsibilities to regulate and make decisions are divided. There is evidence that conflict might arise between national (and sometimes state) policymakers and those leading decision-making in cities in the course of pursuing this opportunity. Much of the activity surrounding regulation and legislation is inevitably led from the national or state level. However, where decisions do not align with local objectives or preferences, there is a risk for conflict, as we have seen in the United States (see section 5.2 in chapter 5).

6.2 PROVIDING THE APPROPRIATE TOOLS AND RESOURCES

This raises questions about what tools and powers policymakers at the city level can access to truly shape the impact that CAVs have on their spatial structures and populations. For many cities, stretched budgets and lack of skills and knowledge can impinge on the ability to respond proactively to CAVs. For instance, net zero objectives are a pressing issue for cities, including how any transition to net zero can be a "just" one and not impose unfair costs on disadvantaged groups.

Table 6.1 Key considerations for policymakers and their potential impacts.

Issues	Considerations	Potential impacts	Possible mitigations
Accessibility and equity	High costs of travel can exclude certain groups of the population	Existing transport inequalities may be exacerbated	CAVs should complement rather than compete with active and public transport policies and infrastructure
Built environment	Possible segregation of different vehicle types and users	Segregation of users can be detrimental if not planned well, e.g., pedestrians are forced to navigate less direct routes to destinations; reduced legibility and permeability of the built environment	Planning new infrastructure to take a people-first approach Requiring CAVs to revert to manual control to enter certain areas
	Intensified use of road space crowds out other road users	Pedestrian and cyclist congestion and conflict. Increase in risky crossing behaviour. Cyclists have greater difficulty in finding and defending road space	Vehicle algorithms cooperate to break up platoons. Junction signals reprioritized to give back space and crossing time to pedestrians and create breaks in traffic flows
Employment and economy	AVs replace human drivers	"At risk" occupations are not replaced by other opportunities creating unemployment issues	Long-term economic development and skills policies to reduce the reliance on logistics sectors
	Spatial impacts of CAVs pushes employment opportunities further from the city centre	Workers forced into longer and more costly journeys. Aggregate vehicle-miles on network increases	Spatial planning policies and practices designed to minimize the need for travel: approaches to density, site suitability for different land uses, transit-oriented development, etc.
Energy and environment	Reliance (at least in the short term) on petrol/diesel vehicles. CAVs produce particulates (tyres, brakes)	Increase in CAVs adds to existing pollution in urban areas	CAV algorithms optimized to reduce tyre impacts and brake wear in urban areas
Health	Increase in sedentary lifestyles with more reliance on private vehicles for individual mobility	Obesity epidemic exacerbated; public health worsened	Complementary active travel and public transport investment
Information technology (IT) infrastructure	Significant investment needed to ensure IT infrastructure able to handle CAV demands	Requirements on local government agencies to improve the physical, software and human infrastructures supporting intelligent transport systems	Ensure new intelligent transport infrastructure are based on open/interoperable standards
	Resilience of vehicle systems and data networks	Safety and congestion issues that result from any systems failure or security breach. Terrorist use of CAVs	Junction and built environment designs with redundancy and "fail-safe" features, including design and technical standards for protecting crowded places

(Continued)

https://doi.org/10.1080/2578711X.2022.2085930

Table 6.1 Key considerations for policymakers and their potential impacts. (*Continued*)

Issues	Considerations	Potential impacts	Possible mitigations
Public engagement	Lack of engagement and dialogue with the public	Public not given sufficient voice in developments around CAVs and their impacts on the built environment. Lack of understanding of the potential benefits leads to a continuance of the private ownership model and less emphasis on shared models. Conflicts over parking and kerb space	Urban parking and street management policies should sensibly anticipate and shape behaviours. Sufficient land and facilities for shared CAV drop-off, parking and circulation
Road safety	Over- or underestimation of the abilities of CAVs to navigate safely, particularly as the technology continues to develop	Increased safety risk to pedestrians, cyclists, etc.	Local and national public education campaigns. Updating road safety curricula within schools, cycling safety courses, driving tests and driver guidance

For some cities, CAVs might be seen as a threat to efforts to enhance the liveability of their environments. Indeed, the literature suggests that places that are already more amenable to motor vehicles are likely to see their populations more willing to travel further because of CAVs.[2] For those places striving to reduce private car dependency, CAVs might be seen as a threat. The arrival of earlier forms of disruptive mobility technology, such as ridesharing platforms, e-scooters and bike-sharing schemes, have all posed regulatory problems for urban policymakers. The challenges and experience of adapting the environment and wider transport network to these is a precursor to some of the inevitable problems that CAVs will bring.

Responding to an increasing presence of CAVs will require wide-ranging actions delivered across different spatial scales. The regulatory environment is currently being developed but there is evidence of potential conflicts between national or state and local governments. The clear demarcation of roles and responsibilities is important, but equally cities must be provided with the tools to fully shape how their transport systems develop. The responsibility for preparing for the arrival of CAVs extends far beyond transport planning and will involve the full range of urban policymaking domains (Table 6.1).

The availability of standardized guidance and ability to share best practice remains underdeveloped, and, for those later adopting cities, more consistent and accessible information will help broaden the extent to which they can engage with these issues. Whilst the public is increasingly exposed to CAVs through trials, there remains a lack of public debate over CAVs and what role they should, or could, play in future transport systems and this is an essential next step.

NOTES

1   Freemark Y, Hudson A and Zhao J (2019) Are cities prepared for autonomous vehicles? *Journal of the American Planning Association*, 85(2): 133–151. doi:10.1080/01944363.2019.1603760.

2   Botello B, Buehler R, Hankey S, Mondschein A and Jiang Z (2019) Planning for walking and cycling in an autonomous-vehicle future. *Transportation Research Interdisciplinary Perspectives*, 1: art. 100012. Doi:10.1016/j.trip.2019.100012.

RECOMMENDATIONS

- **National governments can provide leadership in establishing the regulatory frameworks for connected and autonomous vehicles (CAVs), but they also need to better equip and empower cities and regions to respond to CAVs more proactively.** Governments should provide tools, powers and resources to allow policymakers to respond strategically to ensure CAVs align with, rather than disrupt, their existing policy agendas. As examples, governments should enable local planners to better coordinate policies across existing municipal boundaries, provide more powers over parking regulations and charges, and ensure that active travel policies and funding are part of any package of support provided to help cities accommodate CAVs.

- **It is vital that the sharing of best-practice and knowledge-transfer activities are further enhanced to provide clear and accessible guidance for policymakers less equipped to contend with the arrival of CAVs.** Standardized, simple guidance should be developed by competent national bodies and be flexible to allow for the evolving nature of this field. **Disparate professional bodies will need to work together**—for example, organizations that oversee and support professionals working in transport planning, highways engineering, city planning, housing and urban development, public health, and economic development— should work together to agree shared guidance on preparing for CAVs.

- **Countries of the Global South should be brought closer into the dialogue around the development of CAVs.** For many of these countries, the challenges faced in approaching CAVs can be much greater, and they should have a voice in how this field is shaped.

- **The public must be brought closer into debates around CAVs and what role they should play in a future transport system.** Opportunities should be created to use simulations and trials that demonstrate the realities of CAV deployment and the positives and negatives they might bring.

- **Dedicated support should be provided to cities around the digitizing of services and collection and management of data to support CAVs**. Privacy and cybersecurity concerns are a priority, but local policymakers may not be well equipped to navigate these.

- It is evident that if CAVs follow and reinforce trends in private ownership of vehicles, this could be highly problematic for the transport system and lead to increases in vehicle-miles and congestion. **The public needs to be encouraged and incentivized to shift towards shared models of ownership as part of broader efforts to achieve zero carbon ambitions.**

GLOSSARY

Active travel: A term used to encapsulate modes such as walking, cycling, and other active forms of travel such as running and wheeling.

Artificial intelligence (AI): A term used to encompass technology that can think or act in ways comparable with a human, using its surroundings and other information to make decisions.

Automated vehicles: See *Autonomous vehicles (AV)*.

Autonomous vehicles (AV): Also known as automated, driverless or self-driving vehicles, AVs can undertake driver functions such as steering, braking and acceleration with minimal or no human input, and are able to navigate the environment and other road users. The level of automation influences the degree of human intervention required.

Autonomous Vehicles Readiness Index (AVRI): A proprietary index and report produced periodically by KPMG to assess the preparedness of 30 leading countries involved in the development of AVs according to four pillars: policy and legislation; technology and innovation; infrastructure; and consumer acceptance.

Built environment: The human-made environment, whether in urban or natural settings, that makes up the places where the majority of human activity takes place. It includes buildings and transport infrastructure, as well as "green" and "blue" infrastructure such as parks and watercourses.

Connected vehicles (CV): CVs are those equipped with advanced communication technologies that allow the exchange of information, through different communication channels, between the various elements of the transport system.

Connected and autonomous vehicles (CAVs): A term used to encapsulate vehicles that use both connected and autonomous features. Higher levels of automation involve some interaction with the wider transport network and therefore require connectivity by definition.

Driver-assistance systems: Systems that assist or support people in their driving tasks, such as monitoring the vehicle in relation to its environment, providing warnings and information, and augmenting steering, braking or power inputs to the vehicle (e.g., adaptive cruise control or lane-keeping assist). These do not constitute automated driving features and are at lower levels of the SAE (*q.v.*) framework.

eCall: A European Union (EU) (*q.v.*) initiative to integrate automated collision detection, location transmission and emergency assistance requests in vehicles. Such vehicles are CVs (*q.v.*) by definition. eCall is mandatory in certain new vehicles sold in the EU.

European Union (EU): The EU comprises 27 European countries. The organization helps to govern common economic, social and security policies across these member states.

Electric vehicle (EV): EVs rely on electric motors for propulsion, rather than the internal combustion engine, and therefore removes harmful tailpipe emissions and—if the electricity or hydrogen is generated renewably—reduce the consumption of fossil fuels.

Global North: Those countries largely, although not exclusively, in the Northern Hemisphere, which generally have higher levels of wealth, economic development, and democratic and political freedoms.

Global South: Those countries principally in the Southern Hemisphere that have lower levels of wealth, economic development, and democratic and political freedoms.

Last mile: The short distance between that must be navigated to deliver services/goods to the end user. These journeys can be complex and costly for providers.

Liveability: Conditions within places and communities that enable a decent life within accepted cultural and social norms, including the physical attributes of place, the availability and quality of services, and levels of community cohesion. In many circumstances, environmental sustainability and attention to physical and mental health and well-being will be important elements of liveability.

Mobility as a Service (MaaS): MaaS is the concept that different forms of mobility can be brought together to through digital platforms to offer a single mobility service that is accessible to users on demand. This enables the shared use of vehicles, as opposed to sole private ownership.

Net zero: Goals or policies aimed at substantially reducing greenhouse gas emissions such as CO_2 to quantities that do not add to atmospheric levels. Technologies or processes that are zero carbon will have nil effective emissions, although in transport care must be taken to determine whether this is at the point of use (e.g. "tailpipe" emissions), in the course of energy generation or whole life cycle, which would include manufacturing.

https://doi.org/10.1080/2578711X.2022.2085933

Peak car: The hypothesis that car-miles per capita each year per year have reached a peak and that in future they will not increase further.

SAE Levels of Driving Automation: A categorization of vehicle capabilities with respect to the degrees and characteristics of automation, developed by SAE International (formerly the Society of Automotive Engineers).

Spatial structure: The arrangement or distribution across space of different land uses and activities, and their interrelationships. The patterning and density of housing in relation to workplaces would be one important aspect of urban spatial structure and is an important determinant of the demand for transport.

UNECE: United Nations Economic Commission for Europe—in transport terms, UNECE is the body that services the global regulatory framework for vehicle safety and environmental standards.

REGIONAL STUDIES POLICY IMPACT BOOKS

The RSA's Policy Impact Books form a series of short policy facing books addressing issues of contemporary concern.

The books in this series are commissioned to address topical policy questions of contemporary importance to communities engaged in regional and urban studies issues.

Towards Cohesion Policy 4.0

REGIONAL STUDIES POLICY IMPACT BOOKS

JOHN BACHTLER, JOAQUIM OLIVEIRA MARTINS, PETER WOSTNER AND PIOTR ZUBER

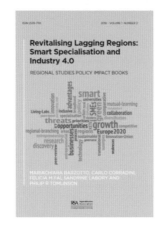

Revitalising Lagging Regions: Smart Specialisation and Industry 4.0

REGIONAL STUDIES POLICY IMPACT BOOKS

MARIACHIARA BARZOTTO, CARLO CORRADINI, FELICIA M FAI, SANDRINE LABORY AND PHILIP R TOMLINSON

Every place matters: towards effective place-based policy

REGIONAL STUDIES POLICY IMPACT BOOKS

ANDREW BEER, FIONA MCKENZIE, JIŘÍ BLAŽEK, MARKKU SOTARAUTA AND SARAH AYRES

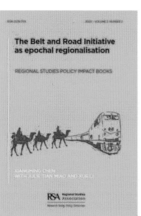

The Belt and Road Initiative as epochal regionalisation

REGIONAL STUDIES POLICY IMPACT BOOKS

XIANGMING CHEN WITH JUCK TIAN MIAO AND XUE LI

Putting universities in their place
An evidence-based approach to understanding the contribution of higher education to local and regional development

REGIONAL STUDIES POLICY IMPACT BOOKS

Louise Kempton, Maria Conceição Rego, Lucir Reinaldo Alves, Paul Vallance, Mauricio Aguiar Serra and Mark Tewdwr-Jones

Levelling up left behind places
The scale and nature of the economic and policy challenge

REGIONAL STUDIES POLICY IMPACT BOOKS

RON MARTIN, BEN GARDINER, ANDY PIKE, PETER SUNLEY AND PETER TYLER

 @regstud

 @RegionalStudiesAssociation

 Regional Studies Association

 office@regionalstudies.org

 www.regionalstudies.org